PN Review 232

VOLUME 43 NUMBER 2 NOVEMBER–DECEMBER 2016

COVER

Alec Finlay, *A Variety of Cultures: An Orchard of Apples & Plums*, Jupiter Artland, 2016. Oak ladders for an orchard of native apples and plums. The ladders anticipate the eventual height of the pruned canopies, and a time when visitors will be able to climb amid the fruit and blossom. Photograph: Ruth Clark. An accompanying book is available from Jupiter Artland.

Editorial

When I was a teacher, a colleague was taken ill and for a semester I covered his Literature classes. He gave me his lecture notes. After having provided the students with his take on the subject, I added my own, suggesting that a variety of differently informed points of view might exist. On his return he was not pleased. For him, the task of examining entailed students knowing and expressing clearly the *correct* answers to questions he carefully anticipated in his pre-examination coaching. He came back in the nick of time to prevent them from making the error of deviation. He had established effective metrics, year on year, for marking, and achieved the 'transparency' committee's love, whatever it cost in fairness to the individual.

Recently I was asked to lecture on Larkin at a local college. I suggested that his poems might be read without continual reference back to his biography, of which the class had been given a sketchy account. At the end of the lecture my host thanked me, then reminded them that they were expected to incorporate biographical information into their exams. Otherwise they would be marked down. Here again were metrics for their intellectual performance, their approach prescribed and standardised.

In one sense it is useful for administrators, teachers, and students to have 'right answers', as in the elementary sciences or elementary history. In another sense it betrays the values that inhere in literary arts and the Humanities at large.

The notion of metrics not only in examining Humanities students, but in the valuation of the works of artists and arts organisations, is spreading. In Australia, the United States, and now in England Arts Councils are developing an expectation of metrics and are supporting research into it. In the new funding round for Arts Council 'portfolio organisations', which will determine the support they receive from 2018–2022, larger clients, receiving £250,000 or more, are required 'to adopt Quality Metrics', the capital Q and M underlining the talismanic importance accorded to this new 'science'. Reassuringly in bold, the power-point slide declares: '**We will not make decisions based solely on Quality Metrics scoring.**' Not *solely*.

Because QM is about scoring, not of effective business structures, professional administration and the like, but of artistic output, misgivings abound. The key 'Research & Development Report' from 2015, available from Arts Council England, is entitled *Home: Quality Metrics*. What might at first surprise the reader is that this initiative is 'sector-led', i.e. the impetus came from Arts Council clients and not from ACE itself. 'Therefore from the outset this has been a sector-led project that has sought to create a standardized and aggregatable metric system measuring what the cultural sector believes are the key dimensions of quality.' It uses 'self, peer and public assessment to capture the quality of art and cultural work'.

These QMs 'aim to help organisations understand what people value about their work, as well as allowing them to benchmark against similar organisations'. With 'what people value' we are entering a curious pseudo-democratic, pseudo-scientific zone in which the measurement of value is conducted by means of a statement with, under it, a line at one end of which is written 'strongly disagree' and at the other end 'strongly agree', with 'Neutral' in the middle. Individuals put an x on the line at whatever point they like. Responses are then 'aggregated' into the Big Data which is the QM Point Score. At no stage are respondents required to deploy language. But so much of the language used in presenting QMs is NewSpeak that it cries out for an Orwell.

The 'core' QMs 'are open source and free for anyone to use'. Here they are, ready for 'Self, peer and public' to strongly agree, strongly disagree, or neither:

Concept: it was an interesting idea
Presentation: it was well produced and presented
Distinctiveness: it was different from things I've experienced before
Challenge: it was thought-provoking
Captivation: it was absorbing and held my attention
Enthusiasm: I would come to something like this again
Local impact: it is important that it's happening here
Relevance: it has something to say about the world in which we live
Rigour: it was well thought through and put together

SELF AND PEER ONLY:
Originality: it was ground-breaking
Risk: the artists/curators really challenged themselves
Excellence: it is one of the best examples of its type that I have seen

Two pilot schemes led to these twelve QMs. In the Executive Summary of *Home: Quality Metrics* we learn that the R&D report was undertaken in Manchester at the initiative of HOME, our new arts precinct, and led by an organisation called 'Culture Counts', joined by academics specialising in Arts Management and Cultural Policy (not in the arts themselves) and in Museology, and a university Museum director. Their objective was to create 'a credible and robust measurement framework for the quality of cultural experiences'. What about the quality of the report's use of English? The style is at once abstract and opaque: 'The novel principle of collaboration and co-production to produce more meaningful data which contributes to a feedback loop for self-evaluation and decision-making is fully adopted by the group of cultural partners in this project, and ostensibly by the wider sector'; and 'there is policy value to arts funding bodies such as Arts Council England, in trialling [sic] quantitative metrics for quality assessment which would be more cost-effective than current peer assessment processes, and which would also avoid the messiness and perceived problems of subjectivity associated with qualitative data'.

The possibility of informed individual judgement (peer review, even) and expertise has gone out the window. They are expensive. That judgement might be something more than, or other than, subjective is no longer entertained. Expertise is a matter of analysis of *post facto* data: it is what you do not with the work being judged but with the averaging out of consumers' immediate responses to it. 'This sector "buy-in" benefits from the scrutiny of a fully tested, robust framework which originated from a reputable consortium of cross-artform partners, working with highly experienced senior arts consultants with industry backgrounds and long track-records, and a technology team [...]' The word 'robust' does a lot of heavy lifting. The artist is replaced by the senior arts consultant with an industry background. The differences that mark books and magazines as cultural products with readers are not considered.

The data collected might allow 'Data Driven Decisions (DDD) to positively shape their cultural and commercial practices'. Here is a vision of the future in which no infinitive is left unsplit: imagine that the 'arts and cultural organisations were measuring the quality of their work using a standardised set of metrics *that they themselves had shaped*' (my italics). Imagine them responding to the instant responses of audiences and end users as recorded on mobile devices, all this occurring 'in real time' through 'an integrated big data platform'. 'The possible prize is to help build a new type of data culture across the cultural sector'. Soon 'the quality of their work' becomes interchangeable with 'the cultural experiences of their audiences and participants'. Facebook and Twitter, instant arbiters, gather mass and force to become the new Maecenases. Another triumph of democracy.

News & Notes

Destination · A most unusual *joint* blue plaque was unveiled at Anne and Vivian Ridler's former Oxford home at 14 Stanley Road on 16 September to celebrate the poet and the Printer to the University of Oxford 1958–1978, who together had such an impact on book culture in the twentieth century. Anne Ridler, a contributor to this magazine, worked on the editorial staff of Faber & Faber, for a time as assistant to T. S. Eliot and later as a freelance reader. She published ten collections of poetry, original and translated opera libretti, and much else. She died in 2001. We understand that in Doughty Street, London, a blue blaque will soon be dedicated to the memory of the poet Charlotte Mew. Women poets are beginning to get their blue due, though there is still some way to go.

David Gascoyne · To mark the centenary of the birth of David Gascoyne on 10 October, Enitharmon Press has published his *Anniversary Epistle to Allen Ginsberg*, a fitting tribute.

Prize-Giving · To those that have shall be given. The Pulitzer Prize-winning poet Sharon Olds has received a $100,000 lifetime achievement purse in the form of the Academy of American Poets' prestigious Wallace Stevens Award for 'proven mastery in the art of poetry'. Now 73, she received the Pulitzer for *Stag's Leap*, a sequence of poems about a divorce, three years ago. Another Pulitzer winner, the former United States poet laureate Natasha Trethewey, was awarded $25,000 and a fellowship. Lynn Emanuel's *The Nerve of It: New and Selected Poems*, took the $25,000 Lenore Marshall Poetry Prize for the best poetry book published in 2015. Donte Collins, twenty years old, received an award for most promising young poet, a prize that has previously gone to Sylvia Plath, Robert Pinsky and Mark Strand.

For her part, Claudia Rankine received a MacArthur 'Genius Grant' of $625,000. She told *Time* that she will use the windfall to establish a 'Racial Imaginary Institute' where 'creative thinkers' can 'come together in a kind of laboratory environment to talk about the making of art and culture and ... the dismantling of white dominance'.

The Pak Kyong-ni Literature Award, in memory of the late Korean novelist Pak Kyong-ni, author of the epic novel *Toji*, and worth ₩100 million (about £70,000) has been presented to the Kenyan novelist Ngugi Wa Thiong'o who, the citation says, 'distinctively reveals different angles of the lives of people undergoing the process of globalization'. The Kenyan 'deeply and fiercely examined and agonized over situations where various boundaries including the West and the Non-West, and modernity and pre-modernity overlap, while dealing with the independence war of Kenya, which became a British colony, and social issues after its independence'. This seems an inspired and timely choice, linking two sides of the cruelly colonized Non-West globe.

This year's Forward Prizes were not without wholesome controversy. Sasha Dugdale's poem 'Joy', originally published in *PNR* 227, received the award as Best Single Poem of the year, and our regular Report writer Vahni Capildeo won the Best Collection prize for *Measures of Expatriation*. 'Because I grew up in Trinidad in the Seventies and Eighties, there was no internet and there weren't many books available to me. It excites me to think that someone who googles 'poetry' – a little reader, such as the girl I used to be – will be able to find it.' Next to the international purses the British purse of £15,000 at first looks modest, but it is less the prize than the recognition it affords that is of value. 'Language is my home, I say; not one particular language.'

The prize for Best First Collection also went to a Caribbean writer, St Thomas-born Tiphanie Yanique, now thirty-eight, for *Wife*, a multi-tonal book about 'the cultural weight of marriage'. 'I'd like to thank my husband for staying with me, despite these poems,' she declared at the prize-giving.

Golrokh Ebrahimi Iraee · On 6 October Amnesty reported the arrest and sentencing of a writer to six years' imprisonment for writing a fictional story about a stoning, a story that she had not even published or circulated to the public. Philip Luther, Amnesty's Director of Research and Advocacy for the Middle East and North Africa, declared, 'she is effectively being punished for using her imagination'. Golrokh Ebrahimi Iraee is a human rights activist as well as a writer. She is accused of 'insulting Islamic sanctities'. Amnesty International suggested, 'Instead of imprisoning a young woman for peacefully exercising her human rights by expressing her opposition to stoning, the Iranian authorities should focus on abolishing this punishment, which amounts to torture. It is appalling that Iran continues to allow the use of stoning, and justifies it in the name of protecting morality.' At the trial, the writer was not allowed a defence; her sentence preceded the hearing, as it were. Her husband too is in detention and has been since June for, in Amnesty's words, 'peacefully exercising his rights to freedom of expression and association'.

Play It Again · The Poetry Archive is a work in progress. It is now offering poets it considers key the chance to record their work again, focusing on later work, thanks to funding from the Garfield Weston Foundation and the Idlewild Trust. Among the poets re-recording are Andrew Motion, Michael Longley, Simon Armitage, Wendy Cope, and Lavinia Greenlaw. A grant from Creative Scotland has facilitated recordings of a range of other Scottish writers, David Kinloch, Anna Crowe and Frank Kuppner among them. The Frank Kuppner recording is likely to be choice and eccentric; those who admire his contributions to *PNR* will certainly await it with bated breath.

Robert Nye (1939–2016) · In *PN Review* 231 we attributed to John Lucas an obituary of Robert Nye which in fact appeared in an extended form in the *New York Times*. Our apologies to both parties for the misattribution. Here is what John Lucas actually wrote.

TUCKED INSIDE THE inscribed copy of *An Almost Dancer: Poems 2005–2011* which Robert Nye sent me was a note. 'This is my last book. (There won't be another.) It might be my best.' He was right on both counts. Although he lived for a further four years there were to be no more publications, but the thirty-three poems that make up *An Almost Dancer* are a perfect distillation of his art. As Helena Nelson, reviewing the book in the pages of *PN Review* commented, 'many of the poems [...] are almost naked in their plainness', but, she added, while their 'themes and motifs are familiar', this a 'patently serious book'. Like Norman Cameron, to whose lyric clarity and teasing, often slant statements Nye owes much, he wasn't a prolific poet, but his devotion to his art was lifelong.

Born in London in1939, Nye left school at the age of sixteen, published his first poems that year in *The London Magazine*, and from then on earned his living as a freelance writer. Regular reviewing for, among other places, *The Scotsman* and *The Times*, where he was a long-serving poetry critic, brought in some money; more came by way of prose fiction. He published collections of short stories, works for children, and a clutch of novels, including *Doubtfire*, *Faust*, *Mrs Shakespeare: The Complete Works*, and *Falstaff*, which won him the Hawthorndon Prize for 1976 as well as the Guardian Fiction Prize. But if his correspondence is to be believed he always found writing prose something of a chore, confessing to a friend that to get started on a day's work he needed Valium washed down with whisky.

Poetry was what mattered, that of others as well as his own. He made discriminative selections of Ralegh, Barnes, early Laura Riding, Dowson; he edited the Faber book of Sonnets; he championed the work of the Elizabethan George Gascoigne, James Reeves, the little-known and soon-dead Clere Parsons, and his friend and mentor, Martin Seymour-Smith. As to his own poetry, *Juvenilia 1*, published in 1961 and warmly welcomed in the *TLS* – 'here is a true poet' – was followed two years later by another *Juvenilia*, and in revised form these were gathered together and joined by more recent poems for his first substantial collection, *Darker Ends* (1969), which won him an Arts Council bursary. Later collections include *Divisions on a Ground* (Carcanet, 1976), *Collected Poems* (Sinclair-Stevenson, 1995), and, from Greenwich Exchange, *The Rain and the Glass: 99 Poems, New and Selected* (2004). There were also some fugitive pamphlets, including *One or Two Swallows* (Eyelet Books/Shoestring Press, 2008), and then the last, beautiful book, published in 2012. He died at his home near Cork, where he had lived for more than twenty years.

Rilke at the Movies · CONTRIBUTED BY FRANK BECK · Rainer Maria Rilke may be one of the twentieth-century writers least likely to appear on a movie screen: his poetry is lyrical, even ephemeral, and not theatrical in the least. Rilke cherished solitude as a vital prerequisite for his work, though it meant living apart from his wife and daughter much of the time. Many of the poet's other important relationships were conducted largely through the mail. Not the stuff of great cinema, one might think.

Despite this, two new German film biographies feature Rilke as a main character. Both focus on the years before the First World War, a time of intense intellectual ferment and flowering artistic creativity. Yet this age of Yeats, Freud, Rodin, Chekov, and Puccini has long been overshadowed by the cataclysm that followed. Now it's ripe for cinematic exploration, and two of Rilke's closest confidantes were important participants in the period: Lou Andreas-Salome, a writer and pioneering psychoanalyst, and Paula Modersohn-Becker, a boldly original artist who challenged ideas about what a woman could paint. Both of these productions were years in the making, the work of filmmakers who hope to reawaken interest in the era. Initial reviews from Europe and North America suggest they are about to succeed.

First to appear was *Lou Andreas-Salomé,* directed by Cordula Kablitz-Post, which opened in Germany in June. A novelist and critic who wrote two early studies of Ibsen and Nietzsche, Salomé later became an analyst to whom Freud sometimes sent patients. The film traces her relationships with Nietzsche (played with gusto by Alexander Scheer), philosopher

Paul Rée, and Rilke; the narrative is framed by her final days in Göttingen in the 1930s, besieged by the Nazis for her association with Freud. Katharina Lorenz and three other actresses share the leading role, one for each stage of life. Kablitz-Post, a noted German documentary filmmaker, co-wrote the script with veteran screenwriter Susanne Hertel.

Julius Feldmeier is their Rilke. We meet him in 1897 as a twenty-one-year-old art history student visiting Munich, where he encounters Lou Andreas-Salomé, an accomplished author of thirty-six. He is immediately smitten. At first she rebuffs his approaches but eventually finds his mixture of diffidence and determination irresistible, and they become lovers. The two were together for just three years, but the bond between them never really ended, as the film makes clear. (Though Rilke and Salomé spent long periods apart, most of the poet's biographers agree that without her guidance and support the *Duino Elegies* and *Sonnets to Orpheus* might never have been written.)

Der Spiegel's review found Kablitz-Post's film 'marvelous' at 'unraveling the tangle of relationships surrounding this rebellious figure'. Austria's *Die Presse* called it 'true to its source and yet – thanks largely to Katharina Lorenz's 'Lou' – incredibly fresh', while Switzerland's *Neue Luzerner Zeitung* said the film 'brings an unbelievable biography thrillingly alive'. It has received eight Austrian Film Prize nominations, including one for Katharina Lorenz for Best Actress.

Christian Schwochow's *Paula* premiered at Switzerland's Locarno Film Festival in August and will come to German cinemas in December. Written by screen veteran Stefan Kolditz and author and theatrical director Stephan Suschke, it tells the story of Rilke's dear friend Paula Modersohn-Becker. In little more than a decade, she grew from a tentative student painter to a Paris-based master who created European art's first nude female self-portraits, before her early death. She was, in one critic's words, 'modern art's missing piece'.

The treatment of Rilke in the two films dovetails nicely, because after leaving Salomé in 1900 the poet went straight to the Worpswede artist colony, near Bremen. Becker was studying there, and this is where Schwochow's narrative begins. His Rilke is Swiss actor Joel Basman, who has to portray both the shy young man who arrived at Worpswede and the more confident person Rilke became, five years later, as Rodin's personal secretary in Paris. Rilke-lovers will notice, however, that, in the first scene in which Basman appears, he recites lines from *Sonnets to Orpheus*, written some twenty-two years after the scene is set. It's a surprising lapse in a film that generally keeps its chronology straight.

Becker is played by Carla Juri, who is also Swiss and has an even more demanding role. We watch her develop from a woman who, as Rilke wrote to Becker's mother in 1916, 'so compliantly and cooperatively devoted herself to family harmony' but who then, 'seized by the passion of her task and renouncing all else, [took] upon herself a life of loneliness and poverty'. Yet the script often presents Becker as a tongue-tied naïf, a figure hard to reconcile with the literate, articulate woman one finds when reading her letters and journals.

Paula has not been widely reviewed yet, but, after its screening in Locarno, *Variety* wrote that the film 'daubs an unexpected range of tones, from the tragically romantic to the jauntily comic, onto the canvas with free abandon' to create 'a lush, involving biopic'. (Trailers for both films are on YouTube.)

Rilke is already the modern Continental poet most frequently translated into English. These two films, expected to arrive in the UK in 2017, shed new light on the pivotal period in which he, Andreas-Salomé and Modersohn-Becker flourished – and which continues to nourish our own.

Bernard Bergonzi (1929–2016) · CONTRIBUTED BY NICOLAS TREDELL · The critic, poet and novelist Bernard Bergonzi died on 20 September at the age of eighty-seven. In fourteen critical books and many essays and reviews, Bergonzi made a wide-ranging contribution to the understanding and appreciation of literary works from the late Victorian to the modern era and engaged thoughtfully with the debates on the novel that enlivened the 1960s and the conflicts over literary theory that galvanized the 1980s. His writing was informed, accessible and, where appropriate, amusing. While he affirmed an English liberal humanist stance as a critic, his Catholicism made him aware of what he called, in his provocative essay 'The Terry Eagleton Story' (first published in *PNR* 40), 'a major world of thought and commitment elsewhere' and enhanced his understanding of both Catholic and Marxist authors writing against the grain.

Bergonzi, a cradle Catholic, was born in Lewisham in London, the son of Carlo, a dance band musician and later white-collar factory employee, and Louisa (née Lloyd). Illness marked his childhood and youth and he came close to death more than once before he reached twenty-one. His early career was chequered; he worked as a clerk but began to earn a reputation as a poet; two of his poems featured in the opening programme of John Wain's radio series 'First Reading', then a cutting-edge platform for what became known as the Movement. His first poetry volume, *Godolphin and Other Poems*, appeared in 1952, and three further volumes followed: *Descartes and the Animals* (1954), *An English Sequence* (1966) and *Years* (1979).

In autumn 1953, supported by a London County Council grant, Bergonzi went to Newbattle Abbey, a residential adult college near Edinburgh, where Edwin Muir was the warden and his English Literature tutor. He returned to London in June 1954, worked as a clerk again and wrote an unpublished novel. Deciding to pursue a university education, he went to Wadham College, Oxford on a scholarship in autumn 1955. His younger fellow students, such as the novelist and historian David Caute, saw him as possessing a portfolio of experience which they lacked. When rogue intellectual Colin Wilson, author of *The Outsider* (1956), visited Oxford, his remark about the critical neglect of H. G. Wells's early scientific romances sowed the seed of Bergonzi's B.Phil dissertation and his pioneering first critical book, *The Early H. G. Wells* (1961).

By then, Bergonzi was a lecturer at Manchester University. His second critical book, *Heroes Twilight* (1965, 1980) is eminently readable and now a classic point of reference in the study of Great

War writing. In 1966, he moved to Warwick University where he remained until his retirement, rising to become Professor of English and serving from 1979 to 1982 as a pro-vice-chancellor.

The Situation of the Novel (1970, 1979) offered, for its time, a state-of-the-art anatomy of the differences between contemporary British and American fiction, contrasting 'The Ideology of Being English' with 'The Incredible Reality' of the USA. Bergonzi grasped why and how the novel, as a form, had buckled in the later twentieth century and if he deprecated some of the more outré attempts to hammer it into new shapes, he gave them fair audience. The book remains valuable for its survey of the state of fiction at a crucial moment and for its insights into a rich range of authors from Anthony Powell to Thomas Pynchon.

Bergonzi's only published novel, *The Roman Persuasion* (1981), evokes an English Catholic community in the 1930s and offers a counter-narrative to the myth of the Spanish Civil War as a struggle between righteous Republicans and nefarious Nationalists. It drew on the family history of his first wife, Gabriel (they married in 1960 and she died in 1984), and on his work on his critical book *Reading the Thirties* (1978).

Bergonzi's other critical books include studies of T. S. Eliot (1972, 1980) and Gerard Manley Hopkins (1977) and a history of English literature from 1939 to 1960, *Wartime and Aftermath* (1993). In 1990, his *Exploding English* gave an absorbing account of the development and current crisis of 'English literature' as a discipline and made the radical recommendation that cultural studies should absorb most of literary studies (including the analysis of prose fiction) and that those really keen to study literature should take a degree focusing on poetry, which Bergonzi called, in his interview in *PNR* 79, 'the most intensive form of literary experience'.

In the twenty-first century, his illuminating biography *A Victorian Wanderer* (2003) charted the geographically and spiritually peripatetic life of Matthew Arnold's younger brother, Thomas. Bergonzi himself remained spiritually constant but kept a low profile about his faith in his criticism, acknowledging in his *PNR* 79 interview that religion was 'important' to him but 'somewhat private'. It is fitting that his final book, *A Study in Greene* (2006), brings together his Catholicism and his liberal humanism in a fine study of a Catholic convert who became a major twentieth-century novelist.

Letters

ROBERT GRIFFITHS WRITES: I enjoyed and admired Duncan Mackay's scholarly piece in *PN Review* 230 (July–August 2016) written partly in reply to my own on the relations, if any, between Einstein's revolutionary work in physics and what I called the 'coincidental' emergence of modernist poetry. Mackay's aim is to bring out ways in which natural science influenced T. S. Eliot more than is generally thought.

Mackay raises interesting questions about the extent to which when a poet is influenced by something to a small extent, how this should be balanced with the extent to which a poet is not at all influenced by the same thing, and how this all should affect our overall conception of a writer.

In general, it still seems right to say that Eliot was not influenced by natural science in any significant way. Essentially, Eliot is a *religious* poet, albeit one struggling to articulate a meaningful sense of spirituality in a world he sees as otherwise bereft of meaning. He is more metaphysical than physical. What I feel is most interesting about Eliot, as a highly educated intellectual at the turn of the twentieth century, is the extent of his lack of interest in natural science, his lack of knowledge of science (which Mackay concedes) and the barest evidence of the existence of natural science in his poetry, and I will venture, humbly, that there is a sense in which this fact is a more important one about Eliot than the not unimportant subtleties revealed by Mackay. It is more important because it gives us a truer sense of what kind of poet Eliot was, as well as a truer sense of what were considered at the time the priorities and possibilities for 'modern' poetry.

My point is possibly only a corollary of the idea, to which the likes of William Carlos Williams subscribed, that Eliot is not really a *modern* poet at all because, unlike the scientist, he is largely looking backwards. Perhaps we only reach truly modern poetry when we find Miroslav Holub, scientist and poet, denying 'spiritual expansion' and for whom the soul has finally given way to the cell.

IAN BRINTON WRITES: I was delighted to see that the volume of essays on *Contemporary Olson* which David Herd edited so excellently for Manchester University Press was given an appropriate sense of space and place in the recent issue of *PNR*. However, it might just be worth pointing out one or two little blips. Referring to the essay about 'In Cold Hell, in Thicket', contributed by Michael Grant and myself, the reviewer suggests that we 'present the poem as comparable to Eliot's autobiographical "The Love Song of J. Alfred Prufrock"'. I am afraid that this is an important misreading of what we said. We refer to the 'significant differences between the modes of these two poems and we must recognise that Prufrock, as subject, is *in* and *of* the poem, an effect of a certain procedure of writing, whereas Olson is present *in propria persona*. His poem is confessional in a way that Eliot's is not [...]'. It might also be just worth pointing out that *Black Mountain Review* was edited by Robert Creeley and not Jonathan Williams, Andrew Crozier was a pupil of Prynne's not a colleague, and that my name is not Briton but Brinton.

Not to Speak a Form of Speaking

VAHNI CAPILDEO

SILENCES HAVE many qualities. When I think of beautifully deployed silences, I think of the *Book of Judith*. Under or against the secular-ish patriarchy (if I may), artists tend to be provoked by the sex and violence of Judith's story, as she goes on a wartime mission to seduce and behead the enemy leader Holofernes. If their delicious Judiths were desserts, they would be red velvet cake. She may be simplified into a 'strong' woman. A few note the cynical exploitation of the young widow: she is used goods, so it all right for her to be further exposed, sent into danger to do the dirty work. One extraordinary silence is Judith's pre-history with her husband Manasses. It is a thing of extremes, sun and suddenness:

> And her husband was Manasses, who died in the time of the barley harvest: For he was standing over them that bound sheaves in the field; and the heat came upon his head, and he died in Bethulia his own city, and was buried there with his fathers. [Judith 8:2–3]

Judith's married life comes to this point. Judith is solar-powered with trauma. Then three years and six months are jumped over, as in a late Shakespeare play. Another silence relates to class. After performing the decapitation (it is specified: alone; two strokes), Judith hands Holofernes's head to 'her maid' and tells her to bag it up. This anonymous and practical person seems to have helped her mistress dress, accompanied her through enemy lines, and transferred domestic skills to the concealment of assassination, returning wordless and unremarked in the outcries of praise for the main heroine. She deserves, perhaps, a poem or a novel of her own. Yet perhaps the most marked silence occurs between Judith 13:10 and 13:11. Before Judith takes physical action, she takes verbal action. She is cited as praying for strength; additionally, words from her prayers are quoted. After the execution, she rolls the head away from the body. It is only 'after a while' that she goes out to deliver the object. That is a moment of total privacy in the text. Word, action, and verse have been completed. Time is understood to pass in the interstice. Judith is absolutely humanly alone with a dead warlord and an invisible Lord.

What about when poets self-silence? Not because of the terrors which cross-hatch some poets' personal life, such as being censored, framed, disowned, tortured, or jailed. Not because your everyday speech is subjected to over-frequent metacommentary, so that your description of which storage jar you put the beans in, or how the spider ran behind the curtain, is met with 'Everything you say is so poetic. Why don't you write about that?', triggering a poetic sulk where you write nothing for weeks. What if Browning had agonised so much that he aborted his *Dramatis Personæ* rather than risk being 'inauthentic' in daring to 'speak for' stranglers, organists, or ancient Greek women? If you are a poet, what excluded poems worry at you, making arguments, tunes and images – poem-ghost-Catherine Earnshaws beating at your window to be let in?

Part of what silences me is the formal education which fostered the illusion that writing had the freedom to be objective, and that emotion could be spontaneous. Like an Isherwood traveller-camera, or like a 'young adult' literature (white) character transformed by a powerful, symbolically creative affinity with the mysteries of a place, person, object or civilisation (of any era, ethnicity or latitude), I believed 'one' would move through life recording, responding, recording responses. *Che bello!* If writerly attitudes were diagnosable DSM psychiatry-style, there would be overlapping lists of characteristics for 'universal value disorder' and 'cultural entitlement disorder'. Instead, whatever I say may be re-presented as representative, of groups I did not represent or backgrounds not germane to the subject. Whatever I say may be used against, or for, others; reapplied wherever there are Others.

Authorship in the age of social media is like an arranged marriage. One cannot fall in love. Depending on one's image / lineage, one can be prised apart from unsuitable liaisons, such as prose nature writing about Yorkshire, which may be suppressed without being publicised, and made to espouse Multi-Postsomethingism. 'Nothing to which UKIP could object,' was someone's gloomy remark after reading, not without enjoyment, yet another svelte volume of pastoral. My cousin, the Canadian writer Neil Bissoondath, did fall in love.

> I will never forget the bright summer evening many years ago when, fresh off the plane from a trip to Europe, I stood on my apartment balcony gazing out at the Toronto skyline, at the crystal light emanating off Lake Ontario and beyond. I took a deep breath of the cooling evening air and knew, deep within my bones, that it was good to be home. [https://newint.org/features/1998/09/05/multiculturalism]

The mildness and predictable cadence of this Happy Homecoming paragraph, however, is ironically revolutionary in context. It is a conclusion to a vexed and vexatious article about diversity, tolerance and false premises. Refreshing in a different way is the Out of Bounds poetry project (see @OoBPoetry). In collecting Black and Asian British place poetry, *Out of Bounds* breaks a silence north, south, east and west: the tacit, retrogressive privileging of some kind of authenticity by olde blood right in nature writing and psychogeography.

Here is a thing I have never written into a poem. It would be mischievously used. It is the experience of wearing a headscarf, which I did voluntarily for a few days when visiting a Muslim family where this was their norm, though not common in their country. My style as a guest is to become as close to invisible as possible, either by going off on my own or by disappearing into the routine of the family, including meal types and activity times. Nocturnal by nature, I liked the challenge of rising early and the spirals of sound in the cool dawns. If I said that when I started wearing it, my friend's attitude to me changed subtly, she might remember otherwise, or claim that I exaggerated or misunderstood: but it was only once I was veiled that she began to administer small, loving scoldings – for walking too fast up the escalator; for wanting to take the stairs instead of the lift down a tower; for saying that menstruation need not be painful (it 'should hurt' because 'something is happening', and it is scripturally designated that women travail). Perhaps this was just a result of growing familiarity. That, of course, is my experience of her reaction to me. I still have not written up the experience of wearing a headscarf. It is difficult for me to hold back, because I am a phenomenological poet, not one of 'identity'. My head was grateful to be shielded from the direct sun, as I have known from looser impromptu veiling in India. My eyes were bothered by the lines at the side of my face. My peripheral vision seemed narrowed, almost in the way it does when I begin fainting (the first time I fainted, it was just like Homer's description of darkness curtaining the field of vision of the wounded). I missed the wind on my hair. I missed the wind on the cilia in the tunnels of my ears. I became hyper-aware of a filtered, felted quality to external sound. The sounds of my body itself seemed amped up. I cannot write this into a poem. It would not be read phenomenologically, as it should be; not alongside my poems about being in water or listening to the night. So here it un-belongs, in prose about the qualities of silence.

Sir Geoffrey Hill

ROWAN WILLIAMS

The following sermon was delivered at the funeral of Sir Geoffrey Hill at the Chapel of Emmanuel College, Cambridge on 25 July 2016.

*

VERY WELL, you shall redirect the pain –
May already have worked this – towards paean.
    Nothing bereaves
    Precisely; yet
    Lost springs of loves
    Turn things about
    Upon the stiff axis
    Geared by bow staves   [*Clavics* 25, p. 35]

'A trimmed rod of wood', says the definition, 'to be made into a bow.' Loss is 'imprecise', nothing serious, grievous, in our humanity allows us the satisfaction of being exact, wrapping it all up. What we do with bereavement is to find words that 'turn things about', labouring at a vehicle where the tension and slowness are in fact building towards an arrow flight.

So today, sitting with our 'imprecise' grief, the loss we can't turn into anything finished and impressive, we listen to Geoffrey's words, in one context after another, burrowing, shouldering, worrying their way towards some redirection of pain. He had characteristically austere things to say about the self-delusions of poets. In a notable essay on 'Language, Suffering, Silence' (*Collected Critical Writings*, pp. 394–406) he conducts several swordfights simultaneously (it is one of the exhausting and exhilarating features of his best critical writing that you have to remember in pretty well every sentence just how many people he is arguing with) – with Arnold, Auden, Milosz, Yeats, all to do with what poetry is meant to do or be in the face of the violation of humanity – or, to paraphrase the question, though still in Geoffrey's own terms, what is the nature of 'ethical' poetry. It is not enough to think of poetry being 'vented' in action; it is not enough to make ironic noises about poetry making nothing happen; not enough to reduce it to the moment of privileged intensity that somehow escapes the wheel of history. It is true that poetry is not 'about' passive endurance; just as true that it is not 'about' inspiring readers to political action, even political violence. And this magisterial clearing of the path leaves one observation standing: Hopkins's comment in a letter to Robert Bridges that the way to respond to suffering is almsgiving, most particularly a resolution to give up buying books for a period and devote the money to the needy. So much for literary eloquence about silence and suffering...

The essay asks for a theology of language. If grace occurs in poetry – 'the abrupt, unlooked-for semantic recognition understood as corresponding to an act of mercy or grace' – we have to see how and why it is simultaneously 'a shock of ethical recognition'. But for that shock to occur, we have to find our way beyond the surface noise of emotion and propaganda and sentimentality. He gently rebukes the great theologian Austin Farrer in another essay (*ibid.*, p. 572) for writing – in a discussion Geoffrey otherwise admires – about 'human existence clamouring for expression'. Clamour is exactly not what brings the ethical into focus. And simply chattering about pain, in prose or poetry, corrupts us, takes our attention away from the imperative of *justice* – a word that has to be weighted both within and beyond aesthetics. As the essay on suffering and silence concludes, aesthetics is a good, but does not save: the weight of the world's stresses has to be carried by means other than poetry alone. Arnold's activism, Auden's irony – both are inadequate. Poetry is a real good, and not the only one. It is an aspect of the hunger for justice. It must do justice in its wording and do what it can to carry stresses that are not only *its* business. And, as he suggests almost casually, one of the most significant ways in which poetry does this is by memorialising the dead. Geoffrey's readers will recognise at once the centrality of this to his own practice: if poetry cannot be either propagandist or exquisite, one thing it is singularly equipped for is doing justice to the past of words and speakers, giving voice in a multitude of ways to that always-present cloud of witness, about whose fate in one sense we can do nothing, yet whose life and voice is in some way in our hands. Writing for the fallen and the unfallen alike, you might say, writing for the dead so as to write for the survivors who may not even know what they have survived. Ethical poetry comes slowly into focus as a practice that embodies *witness*, standing consistently in a place where something is, however intermittently, clear, and refusing those versions of it that are slanted by transient feeling, 'agendas' of one kind or another, functionalist reduction or aesthetic over-ambition. The dead won't reward you; so you can write about them without twisting yourself around the politics of a relationship, and simply work for their voice.

And, needless to say, this witnessing entails bearing witness to your own imperfection of witness, your own seductions and dramatisations. Geoffrey's late collections, certainly from *Speech! Speech!* onwards, are characterised by savagely ludic self-chastisement: some of it a pre-emptive strike against the hapless reader or the snide critic, sometimes a rueful fingering over the near-flawless lyric voice of his earlier work, sometimes simply a caricature of the grumpy old man persona – all worked through with comprehensively unmerciful clarity. One of his own most persistent themes, from that wonderful inaugural lecture in Leeds in 1977, is how we 'word' repentance, particularly in the face of that moment where the unmoral is suddenly caught up in the moral – where, in the language he uses later, the simultaneity of semantic and ethical recognition is inescapable; when doing justice in words is transparently bound up with doing justice to what there is in every sense (including what there is, uncomfortably, unreconciledly, inside the poet).

Geoffrey believed that the Christian narrative of guilt (true not self-dramatising guilt, the weight of the stresses born out of one's own failure), of the clarification of our being by grace, of the continuous tension between love and betrayal and of the inexhaustible resource of patience underpinning all things was a narrative that was worth committing to, and it is this that gives us our words today for redirecting pain towards paean, turning things, making our bereavement a little more precise – that is, doing justice to where we find ourselves. We are here because we have all sensed something of our judgement in Geoffrey's words, in poetry and prose: we have been called to account, *brought to justice* as the old phrase has it. We can read the later collections, that extraordinary last flowering of energy and technical brilliance, feeling sometimes that what he says 'chides us beyond all bearing' (*Odi Barbare* XLIX, p. 57) – sets an impossible level of compression, needling challenge, ruthless scrutiny of every syllable, ruthless dismantling of settled and accessible meanings. But these poems are not an aberration: they are fraught with that stress of looking for justice and so inviting judgement on any or all of us who work in words. And they are as much as ever a territory in which grace, ethical and semantic recognition, springs into life again and again.

I have ridden out one cosmos already,
Manner of speaking. The metaphysical
End of desire is always to be real;
The word and world well-met and going steady.

If this is not possible, trick is to renew
Batteries of arcane matter: fatalism
For one; the labyrinth or chasm
Of language. Tedium can be made to glow.

Comes real at last only renunciation.
I am before that, inadequately tired;
What has been taken remains unrestored.
Each word excruciate in its computation.

Command I spit upon clay to obtain merit –
For what remains to us in the great set
Book of the People that is not escheat? –
Who once could beget love but could not bear it.
[*Al tempo de' tremuoti*, 928–9]

Poetry like all speech ends in renunciation; the great set book contains nothing that is not bound to revert to another's ownership. What we say is an attempt to open eyes, as Christ did with the clay and spittle laid on the blind man's eyes; but can we bear what is uncovered? Doing justice is a dangerous enterprise, dangerous for our fragile selves, wounding us and those we love when we cannot bear the weight we have loosed and allowed to slip onto our backs. Geoffrey knew all this, and if his knowing was often angry, that anger was not the final motor of the poetry: not something 'clamouring for expression' but the deeper knowledge of what the subterranean shifting of 'lost loves' and half-lost guilts might bring to birth – or not, of course, because successful 'voicing' is not granted automatically to anyone.

But he has brought something to birth for all of us, by that grace he celebrated, something inescapably *ethical* in a way given to few poets of our age. Here we are to try and echo both the turning of things about in words and the renunciation he spelled out for us. Our bereavement has various levels of imprecision; Geoffrey's family will have a different sort of precision in their grieving, and they will have words for it that the rest us can't share. But in this liturgy we prepare ourselves for the stiff axis of the death and resurrection of Christ to stand steady as we wind our tensions around it and pray for freedom like the arrow's flight, for Geoffrey and for all of us.

Letter from Wales

Sam Adams

AT THE BEGINNING of the 1960s, in the absence of any formal interest on the part of university departments here in what has since become known as 'Welsh writing in English', it was left to Roland Mathias to cultivate an almost entirely neglected field. As editor of that quarterly doorstop *The Anglo-Welsh Review*, he led the way in writing carefully considered reviews of books by Welsh poets and authors and long editorials and critical articles that set the standard for later academic studies. His influence can be seen in the emulative efforts of *Poetry Wales*, founded in 1965 by Meic Stephens and edited by him. Stephens, too, sought to expand reviewing beyond scant notices of recent publications to close scrutiny and assessment, and in those special numbers of the magazine devoted to individual writers (Dylan Thomas, R. S. Thomas, David Jones), to which Mathias usually contributed, gave academic critics, like Jeremy Hooker and Anthony Conran, the opportunity to begin building a conspectus of the subject on scholarly lines. To their lasting shame, neither the then federal University of Wales, nor any of its constituent colleges, awarded Roland Mathias the honour he so richly deserved, but before the end of the century, the seeds he planted, nurtured by gifted scholars of the calibre of M Wynn Thomas, had established Welsh writing in English as a course of study available to students. The metamorphosis of *Welsh Writing in English: A Yearbook of Critical Essays*, which began appearing in 1995, to the *International Journal of Welsh Writing in English* in 2013, is an indication of the subject's status in Wales and in universities overseas.

It still has a long way to go to make any impression on English studies in England, as on the stone-faced or arrogantly dismissive metropolitan media – which is a pity, because it throws up curiously absorbing Welsh-English interests. Almost forty years ago, Roland Mathias, in the way he had, invited me to interest myself in Thomas Jeffery Llewelyn Prichard, and see if what I found might suit *AWR*. After a stint turning over old books and a surprising hoard of manuscripts at Cardiff Central Library I produced an article that corrected the Prichard entry in the *Dictionary of Welsh Biography*. I have written extensively on this topic before (*PNR* 192, 2010) and will not repeat myself aside from mentioning that he wrote what was at the time greeted as 'the first Welsh novel in English', *Twm Shôn Catti* (1828), had earlier been an actor in the London theatre, lost his nose somewhere, and died in Swansea in 1862 after falling into his own fire. As an antecedant of the present race of Welsh writers in English, he is now attracting the attention of academic critics, who tend to focus their attention on the novel, which was Prichard's greatest success. Indeed, having made a little money from the initial publication, he expanded it considerably for a second edition (1839), and at the time of his death was working on a yet longer version, which was eventually published in 1873.

Even allowing for this unfinished attempt at the 'triple-decker' of his dreams, to be auctioned among a score of competing publishers, he probably wrote more poetry than prose. I have taken pains to read all I could, but for the best part of the several decades Prichard and I have been acquainted I have chafed at my inability to obtain a copy of one of his books of poems. I knew it existed because he referred to it on the title page of another publication, *Mariette Mouline*, where he declares himself 'Author of "My Lowly Love," "Theatrical Poems," &c.', but as none of the great libraries of the land possessed a copy of T. J. Llewelyn Prichard's 'Theatrical Poems' I gave it up as lost – several times. Knowing how lost stuff sometimes reappears, I recently approached the National Library at Aberystwyth and asked them to try again. On this occasion, my request reached Martin Riley, senior enquiries assistant at the library, and as usual he drew a blank. Then he searched simply for 'Theatrical Poems' and produced an unexpected result. Yes, the library had a copy of 'Theatrical Poems', not by Prichard, but Jeremy Diddler. This had come to the library in the collection of Joseph Joseph (fl. 1855–1890) and his grandson Capt. James Buckley (1869–1924) of Castell Gorfod, St Clears, Carmarthenshire. Joseph had roots in Brecknockshire, Prichard's home county, and had taken the trouble to bind Jeremy Diddler's slim volume with Prichard's *My Lowly Love*. So there we had it: Diddler was Prichard by another name. When he began to publish poems, in a short-lived magazine *The Cambro-Briton*, he used the *nom de plume* 'Jeffery Llewelyn', which he later incorporated into his own, plain Thomas Prichard. He was not averse to appearing in disguise, and in this case he might have thought it wiser, because most of the poems in the book are satires of contemporary actors and theatre managers and their devious practices. A self-confessed admirer of Charles Churchill (1732–1764), when he compiled the collection, he almost certainly had in mind the latter's *The Rosciad*, originally published anonymously in 1761. The name Jeremy Diddler he borrowed from the chief character in a popular farce of the period, *Raising the Wind*, by James Kenney (1780–1849), first produced at Covent Garden in 1803. 'Jeremy' is a conman, whose aim in life is to marry an heiress. When we are taken in, deceived by a trickster, and say we have been 'diddled', we owe the word to him, or rather to James Kenney who created the character. Prichard had in mind a particular revival more than a decade later when the lead role was played by Richard Jones, to whom *Theatrical Poems* is dedicated.

In the Writers of Wales monograph *Thomas Jeffery Llewelyn Prichard* (UWP, 2000), I proposed that he acted at Covent Garden as 'Mr Jefferies', sharing the stage with celebrated players of the stature of John Philip Kemble and his even more famous sister, Sarah Siddons. In the absence of proof, doubts have been cast on the hypothesis. It was pleasing to find in this late discovery support for my case (in addition to the circumstantial evidence adduced previously). Satire was ever Prichard's strongest suit and anger the inspiration. The most vitriolic attack in *Theatrical Poems*, in a poem entitled 'A Wise Man, A Fool', is aimed at someone he knew well:

Ch---- Kl----'s but a sorry actor,
A fop by art, a fool by nature,
A grovelling squab in form and feature: –
That he ne'er play'd a single part
Consistent with dramatic art,
Except, perchance, once in his noon
Whil'st Covent Garden's pantaloon.

It is not exquisite verse making, but it is deeply felt. A little research identifies the target: Charles Klanert, and a collection of Covent Garden playbills reveals a curious, reiterated juxtaposition. At the opening of the 1805/6 season, in the cast of *The Padlock*, a 'musical farce', we see 'Scholars, Mess. Klannert and Jefferies'; in *Hartford Bridge* they are paired as 'Waiters'; in *Othello* Klanert plays Antonio, Jefferies Julio; in *Hamlet* (20 March 1806), Rosencrantz is played by Klanert, Guildenstern by Jefferies. In these and many other examples the size and importance of the roles are very similar. All are minor. It might be objected that Prichard, born 1790, would have been only fifteen in 1805/6. But youth was no impediment to a stage career. Many major actors of the period began as children: in the production of *Hamlet* noted above, the leading role was taken by 'Master Betty', a fourteen-year-old phenomenon.

From the Journals of R.F. Langley

THE POET R. F. LANGLEY (1938–2011) was also, privately, a prolific prose writer. Extracts from his journals, which he began in 1969, first appeared in *PN Review* in 2002. The notes to Langley's *Complete Poems*, edited by Jeremy Noel-Tod, cite a number of unpublished journal entries that directly informed the writing of his verse.

23 August–7 September 1974, Gislingham Church, Suffolk

The diamond panes in windows have been partly replaced by clear glass, so that one doubts there is glass at all in these random patches. Quilted hotchpotch like the floor. Outside ice clouds pile across and sweep by. The nettles and burnt grass and blackened umbellifers are deep. The sills are below their heads. Looking out from the long hulk of the church, one is low in the water. Mountain ash thrash, elders, some sort of shining leaved bush... it's a spindle tree... meadow cranesbill bleaches white against the footings. Through the back, south window air comes. A hole. And the electric light in a crockery shade, creaks on its long chain. A blue tit climbs on it. Best of all a spotted flycatcher is in the roof, with a nest in an oak hole at the base of the second hammerbeam back on the south of the nave. The bleached, hacked wood warps apart. Dark ground of timbers with newer, browner, shinier replaced boards above in the interstices. Web threads hang weighted with bits and flakes. A burr of wings. The neatness. The worried tail, wet white chin and throat, pale eyestripe, more chestnut back; dark, big eye, and maybe lavender mauve, some plum-like hue misted over the whole, from scarce seen striations on the chest. The path to the nest from the rear window, along the middle air... time for three bursts of wings. Then arrival on a rusted metal rod across under the roof. From there to the top of the embattled hammerbeam, walking there, cocking and peering and cheeping confidentially, watching us for a long time before dropping down into the knotted hole where the profile of the head bobs, feeding, beakfuls of crane flies, a grub, very quickly, then back. The battlements repercuss, ranges of them on the cornice of the roof, on the double layer of hammers, in each window as the three-part, stepped transom effect in the head. In these cities the bird hurries. Blues and browns, creams and reds, refine, fine out in her live shift. A white mute is dropped. The chancel corbel figures, knob-eyed men holding shields, scrolls and musical instruments, glower. One is proud. Another cynical with a trenched sneer and thick lips, deep-socketed eyes and hunched round a big rough lute, stubbed hands grip and bang. Rubbish hangs on them in strings, badges of birdlime in small shot bursts, furred lines of web, spinning flakes of plaster. They scowl. Hands have been smashed off. They are chopped, clawed, split and filthy.

Letter from the Patent Office

P. C. Evans

'*A sentence is condemned to stay as stated.*' SPENDER

I FIRST RAN ACROSS Rilke in Stephen Spender's *Autumn Day*; was lured to Lorca by Spender's renderings also. His restrained translations may have done Lorca a biggie in the forties when there were only so many *ay ays* that Trevor Howard's Blighty could take amongst the carumphing of the whizzbangs. Spender translated Rilke *ganz alleine*, having picked up the lingo while cruising the Weimar; for Lorca, he called in the Catalan cavalry in the form of J. L. Gili. *Autumn Day* is credited to Rilke; the Lorcas bear Spender and Gili's unassuming monikers, Lorca's name is emblazoned in red on the white cover, like the aftermath of a fascist drive by.

We fast forward to 2006, and Faber rains on Rilke's parade, downsizing him to a Don Paterson 'literal', and he doesn't even make it onto the cover of Paterson's *Orpheus*. How do a poet's 'versions' come about? Paterson reads '*echt deutsch*', if I'm not mistaken, and concedes to 'stealing' from more pedestrian translators, who he cites after blowing their efforts out of the water. So, why would one soup up an old jalopy like Rilke and take it out for a spin? Because it adds a showcase of tasteful bric-a-brac to one's own *oeuvre*. When we read *Cathay*, *Imitations* or *Orpheus* we are being invited to consider the poet's trans-versions as equal to, or better than, the original, the poet's liberties often some of their most memorable lines. One thinks of Lowell's 'vermin, jackals, panthers, lice / [...] snatch and scratch and defecate and fuck / in the disorderly circus of our vice'. But, these cameo trysts are not the dutiful grind of the translator's matrimony to his craft.

Allen Prowle recently won The Spender Prize for his translations of the Dutch poet Rutger Kopland. I was curious about someone who I'd never heard of, who'd never translated anything from Dutch, but had won a big prize at his first attempt. The Embassy in London had pasted a link to the Spender Trust's announcement. They also linked to the Dutch originals on Poetry International Web which featured previously-published translations of the same poems by James Brockway and Willem Groenewegen. What struck me, aside from the similarities, was Prowle's reproduction of specific translation choices and even Brockway's occasional mistakes. Prowle's translations had come about by 'piggybacking', switching a synonym here, tidying up a phrase there, so that 'incomprehensible' becomes 'unfathomable', 'silly lions' become 'pathetic lions', but the basic structure remains the same.

James Brockway was an accomplished translator, his translations of Kopland the culmination of his life's work. He spent decades collaborating with Kopland, helping to build his reputation abroad. Groenewegen is another lifer, and collaborated with Brockway in his final years.

Prowle mentions coming across Kopland's poetry in Brockway's translation and admiring the 'parlando style'. He wasn't deterred by not knowing the language: after all, he had Google Translate and two specialist translators who'd done the legwork for him, and he used their translations as his 'literals'.

So, I dropped Groenewegen a line and he got in touch with the Spender Trust. In the meantime, the press got wind of it and whipped the affair up into another plagiarism scandal. What did strike me, amidst the ponderings of the British chatterati in various comment sections, was the conviction that one translation must inevitably closely resemble another. But when you translate from a language of half a million words into a language of one and a half million words, you expect considerable divergence. There will be several English synonyms for most Dutch words. This expectation is increased when you consider the translator's choices: will they adhere to the 'literal' meaning of the poem? What if the poet means two or three things at the same time; which do you choose? What if rhyme, alliteration and consonance are crucial, as with Kopland? How far does one deviate from 'literal' meaning to reproduce elements of form? But first of all, does the translator have the poetic and technical skills to render the original?

The Spender Prize's judges stated that any of Prowle's translations could have won the prize. One judge wrote of never previously having heard of Kopland. With a Harvill *Selected*, a tour of the UK with Seamus Heaney, and reviews in the *Guardian* and elsewhere, he was hardly hiding his light under a bushel. Anyway, the judges awarded a prize for the translation of a poem by a poet they hadn't heard of, from a language they did not understand, to a translator with no understanding of the original language.

For the record, this is a more accurate report: Prowle's winning translation isn't very good and neither is Brockway's, for these reasons. In long English sentences, we place shorter clauses at the beginning, longer clauses at the end. Dutch does the opposite. The first verse of Kopland's poem is a grammatical sentence. Five sub-clauses are followed by a main clause which contains the denouement of the verse, a rhetorical question that lends the poem its poignancy: 'how else am I supposed to have felt, back then, when he closed the doors on her and me'. Brockway, and his shadow, Prowle, lose themselves in an ungrammatical mishmash. The sentence's complexity lures even the experienced Brockway into a grammatical mistake; Prowle lacks the language skills to make the same mistake.

A lot is going on beneath Kopland's 'parlando' veneer which both translators fail to comprehend. They reduce the poem's tone to that of a timeworn anecdote, where the Dutch is concise, suggestive and imbued with a sense of identification and loss. Both translators lose the poem from the very first word: 'vroeger'. 'Vroeger' literally means 'earlier'. But the Dutch have forty meanings for 'vroeger'. Synonyms include a thesaurus-full of poetry killers, but 'vroeger' is a common two-syllable word that doesn't immediately draw a yawn. Brockway's 'In those days' and Prowle's 'Back then' lack Kopland's *codensare*, as well as the alliteration of 'vroeger' and 'vader' (father), the consonance of 'vroeger' and 'groot' (big), the melancholy trochees of 'vroeger' and 'vader', and the catch in the breath as the line breaks on 'was' (a technique that Kopland uses again in verse three with 'uit' (out)). What's more, the opening lines should be a couplet to emphasise the line break.

To ensure that the poem has no chance of surviving the translator's operating table, these two translators dip into their lucky bags of Housman-esque poetasters' vocab and resort to hackneyed poeticism: 'suddenly as old as he', 'my father towered still', 'separable no more', Brockway's 'persons unknown', and thus Prowle's 'people unknown', for the common word 'strangers'. These translators fail to grasp the style and tone of Kopland's poem. Lowell writes: '...in poetry tone is of course everything'.

To his credit, Prowle does engage with the original too. He changes Brockway's wordy 'the shuffle of mother's slippers' to 'mother's sad shuffling', which he believes to be closer to the Dutch. However, he doesn't realise that the Dutch word 'sloffen' is both the verb 'to shuffle' and the plural of 'slof/slipper'. Hence Brockway's clotted line. Prowle follows Kopland's line break on 'dead- / still house'. What he couldn't know is that 'doodstil' is a commonplace Dutch word that every Dutch poet, in every poem about death, breaks at the end of the line. And though unoriginal, the word isn't as contrived as the melodramatic 'dead / -still house'.

What is the plagiarist's motivation? If one isn't going to make it new, why make it at all? It isn't as though there are real financial or reputational benefits. And Prowle's mugshot doesn't quite fit the Wanted poster. When he began 'translating' Kopland, I believe he thought he was doing so as a poet: re-crafting lines and selecting 'better' synonyms, and some of his lines are indeed more evocative than Brockway's, but they could not have existed independently of Brockway and Groenewegen. Hubris may have suggested to him that he was working from 'literals', not the crafted versions of seasoned and widely-published translators. It didn't occur to Prowle that he might be infringing copyright and passing off their work as his own.

Prowle's reputation is now damaged, though he did creditably withdraw his translations and donate his prize money to charity. I am sure the Spender Trust is now aware that Prowle's practice is not consistent with its mission of honouring Stephen Spender as a champion of the rights of creative artists. They have tightened up their rules and procedures for this year's prize.

Publishers and organisations who take a punt on foreign poetry are thin on the ground in the UK. Particularly as the cavalcade of myopic Kippers contemplates the obscure reveries of the inward gaze, we need organisations like the Spender Trust and the spirit of Stephen Spender.

Caroline West's 'Chesil Bank Fall'

TOM LOWENSTEIN

CAROLINE WEST wrote 'Chesil Bank Fall' in 1961 and it was published in *Pawn*, a poetry magazine edited at Kings, Cambridge by Richard Boston and Corin Redgrave that summer. The poem is one of seven pieces that Caroline wrote and published when she was a student at Cambridge and which I collated for private publication in April 2016. The booklet is dominated by Caroline's majestic long poem, 'In the Same Night', which was published in *Granta* in 1961.

At a *Granta* event the same summer I overheard Muriel Bradbrook, Caroline's tutor at Girton, remark in her disarmingly donnish way, 'Of course Caroline's working on the threshold of a precocious genius... And I'll never again say the word *no*.' (This in reference to Caroline's satirical use of the word *no* in her poem.) It was encouraging to hear this endorsement of Caroline's originality, although Caroline herself deprecated her work and lost confidence in her creativity.

Caroline West was born in 1941 and grew up in the west of England. Her grandparents were Rebecca West and H. G. Wells, both of whom she knew in their old age. In 1960 Caroline started an English degree at Cambridge and graduated in 1963. In 1970 she went with her husband, the late Osei Duah, to work on an agricultural project in Ghana. Following a serious breakdown, she returned to the UK where she lived in Dorset. Osei continued to develop a distinguished career as an agronomist and divided his time between Ghana and the home he later shared with Caroline in Lewisham.

Caroline was, in 1960, a profoundly modest and unostentatious person and it remains a source of wonder to me that she had even heard of *Granta*, let alone the *Granta* Freshman's Poetry Competition which she won (from David Frost, editor) with two short poems published in the 2016 booklet.

I lost touch with Caroline after we left university, but we met briefly some time in the 1970s and she sent me some new poems when I was in Alaska. Unfortunately I've mislaid these and the seven pieces in the 2016 booklet represent the totality of her published work.

'Chesil Bank Fall' is one of Caroline's most remarkable and characteristic poems. The lyricism is painterly and hermetic and this is balanced by an evocatively disjoined narrative which conflates a beach scene with children and a personal encounter at once subjective and distanced by adult memory. The anonymity and naturalism of the encounter, at once sensual and, in a remote way, mystical, takes on a contemplative historical retrospective symbolism as children, framed by the freedom of play on the beach, themselves fringe a crucial moment of implied sexuality, and the scenario thus layered, is set against the sombre ending.

These levels of evocation are themselves conveyed within the poem's two more or less equal sections. Section I is controlled by a simple rhythmic syncopation and held in place by the lovely, casual painting in of images of the 'eyes' and 'hand' which have their place there. This quiet, marine opening is both echoed and contradicted by the final beautiful stanza of Section II. Here the 'hand', which had 'slipped' from momentary adult control at the opening, is let fall, at once disengaged and observantly conscious 'when he / Stopped'. Death, with grotesque but sacramental formality, is evoked: prematurely but with a chilling, introverted comprehension.

Caroline, who is now severely disabled, sent me handwritten copies of seven more recent poems. Here is one which courageously expresses thoughts and feelings about her condition:

THE FIERY SPIRIT

This thing that walks about and falls,
That takes up space and waits for meals,
Whose eyes are dim, whose voice a croak,
Whose mind confuses day with night –
Bereaved, unloving, full of fears –
Sleep fitful,
Thirst perpetual,
Deafness imminent –
'Old thing', 'Poor thing' –
Have none of it.
The fiery spirit is victorious.

And here on the right is Caroline's 'Chesil Bank Fall'. For a copy of Caroline's 2016 booklet, write to tlowenstein@blueyonder.co.uk or anthony.rudolf@menardpress.co.uk.

Chesil Bank Fall

I

The children scattered on the graded
Pebbles.   The dog slid.   The tamarisks whipped.
My eyes watered, and that made it
Worse, when my hand slipped

And
    conscious of nothing but your concave
Let the wind take
                        ribs and joint stones grating

    the dried grasses we'd meant to save
Particularly
            under joint weight.

The children came back, their pockets gourded
Down with glass, feathers, shells, and bones.
Replacement for grasses? not important what's hoarded?

Exploded in our fire. Any
Place you sat, the smoke was blown,
And tinged like the questions raised by many
Of the sea things I now own.

II

Will your green eyes rub as opaque
As this once clear, much jostled glass has?
Will constant see-saw actions break
Us open to the passes

Of indiscriminate blue-lit hordes,
With passage of which kind of creature
This unhinged bivalve's look accords?
Will we, devoid of feature
As this fragment of some once white shell
(Merlin's current money, marked
with purple), show our veins as well?
We ate.   The dog barked.

I found myself tracing spirals when he
Stopped. The sky had turned stormy and brown.
Whose second eye should this greened penny
Abrasively close down?

From the Archive

Issue 132, March–April 2000

ALISON BRACKENBURY

From a contribution of six poems. Fellow contributors to this issue include Anne Stevenson, Jeremy Over, Robert Bly, Jeremy Hooker, Ruth Padel, and Christopher Middleton.

HOLIDAY

Christmas. I go back to bed with a fig
Whose belly is plump and swollen with seeds,
Crisp, gold as small fires, yet in each one
Is something dark and thick, which needs
To linger and be kept with care.
For the days are short, then the mornings start
Darker, as we freeze and work.
Earth fills the seeds at the lost fig's heart.

Become a subscriber and gain unlimited online access to the entire *PN Review* archive spanning over forty years.

An Unforgettable Series of Journeys on the Glasgow Underground

FRANK KUPPNER

30 · Also, Leo, as I rather think I was just saying, one might learn [more] about the allegorical element – and then wish one *hadn't* done so: perhaps because the allegory as such is so strained or uncongenial to one's own world-view? (But I dare say the word 'good' ['good allegory'] is there to allow one the bargain value-for-effort / ergonomically highly efficient resource of claiming that any allegory in which such considerations obtain cannot, *ipso facto*, be a good one.)

31 · After all, is one really to doubt that one gains more pleasure from such propositional content as a poem might contain if and to the extent that one shares the beliefs that are expressed in it? Or is there an equal (surely not greater?) pleasure in thinking something along the lines of: 'Beautifully put – but, no: I don't agree with that [at all]?'

32 · Much as, say, an artful, brilliantly evoked description of so-called 'time-travel' – literally travelling into the somehow-right-here past – might be to those who think there is in principle not even the remotest chance of such a thing being possible, never mind actual. No matter how wondrous might be the impossiblist verbal or situational effects achievable thereby, a sort of near perpetually distantly-clanging sense of '*Yes, but*' will hang over the whole wondrous body even so. Every moment of the experience is horribly vulnerable to the deflating thought: 'But this simply couldn't happen, Jim!'

33 · Or perhaps it is as if one should *suspend judgement* (or some such) in the salient passages of a poet who *genuinely believed* that, say, the Jews were more or less behind all of it – lest a more unsuspended approach might to some extent blind one to the verbal or conceptual majesty of what (else) might be going on? But the fact that [some of] the core beliefs are, to say the least, absurd, is itself part of what is actually going on here for that particular interpreter – just as much as any genuine glory, majesty and might might be. (Yes. (What? Might it *not*?))

34 · (After all, Beat-rice, surely content is something more than a sort of arbitrary element of book design?)

35 · Or does this perhaps take things to too intense a level of discomfort? Is it merely that, when listening to a fantasist or a fabulist, one ought in principle to believe him – but perhaps then suspend belief when he starts to argue [for] something that one is as certain as can be (or whatever) could not for a moment possibly be true? (In order that one might be left free to appreciate more fully the glory of his (technically, often untrue – not to say, in any mundane sense, utterly incredible) utterance?)

36 · (Of course, I am talking here of things which are supposed to hold good in the real world; of whatever is supposed to be true there. Leaps of imagination, whimsy, ludic indulgences, 'mere entertainment' and so forth are all very nearly quite another matter.)

37 · But, no: there the statement is anyway, in black and white, with a comparatively unusual directness for Eliot: 'I deny, in short, that the reader must share the beliefs of the poet in order to enjoy the poetry fully.' As it stands, this contention strikes me as being simply and obviously untrue – though no doubt a certain amount of room for manoeuvre may again be available to one in suitably sophisticated treatments of the meanings of 'fully' and, perhaps even more so, 'enjoy'. Might Eliot, for instance, have let the verb 'enjoy' take over from 'understand' while his sublime and, by the sound of it, more or less *infallible* attention was momentarily directed elsewhere? (Replace 'enjoy' with 'understand' and his assertion, I think, becomes true.) If not, are we really to suppose that there is not a sort of distinctive overplus of enjoyment to be had from reading something which seems to catch wonderfully well (and such a rare delight too!) beliefs that one shares, views that one [utterly] agrees with? [Hmm ... Sorry to insist on the point, Your Reverence – but I'll have to raise you all-in on that particular hand. (*Of course* there is!)]

38 · 'If you deny the theory that full poetic appreciation is possible without belief in what the poet believed, you deny the existence of 'poetry' as well as 'criticism'. Better not dare then, eh? Just you try it and see what happens! The big, strong man will get very angry with you – and he *knows* people; some very *important* people indeed. Yes. Minor royalty; Provençal speakers; really powerful guys from Harvard – all that sort of thing.

39 · (Even so, the Oracle does seem to be a bit loose with his terminology. Again, if 'appreciation' means 'understanding', I should say the theory is true. If it means 'enjoyment' then I dare say it might well be true to some extent – but, the more unattractive one finds the belief, the less one is likely to appreciate its expression.) (Still. The quotation-marks around 'poetry' and 'criticism' are a nice magisterial touch. I suppose he merely means, poetry and criticism *tout court*? (He's not actually quoting anyone else, is he?))

40 · But anyway: here we have a man – if he really is only a man – who can use the phrase 'full poetic appreciation' with the voice of one who is familiar with this obviously sublimely elevated phenomenon. No mere 99% or so for the Captain! How wonderfully the gaps (or, indeed, the complete absence) of argumentation may be made up by sheer overbearing assertion, if only the knack has once been acquired. 'And if you push this denial to its conclusion, you will be forced to admit that there is very little poetry you can appreciate, and that your appreciation of it will be a function of your philosophy or theology or something else.' (Got that much at least, Pard?

Reading Wordsworth

Two poems from *Lyrical Ballads* (4th edition, 1805)

THOMAS KINSELLA

READING 'NUTTING'

Lines 1–3: High expectations established: 'singled out'; 'heavenly'; immortality;

4–7: followed by ordinary rural matters in plain narrative: the speaker setting out for a day gathering nuts in the distant woods.

7–13: He sees himself as faintly comic, with marks of the beggar and clown; dressed for the roughnesses ahead by his attentive, sensible wife.

13–20: Reaching the distant woods, he finds a sheltered, virgin scene waiting, untouched. He senses its vulnerability, and there is an atmosphere of threat in the words 'broken', 'Drooped...withered', 'ungracious', 'devastated'.

20–24: His response is intense: paused; standing and observing, almost breathless with pleasure; controlling his great emotion while indulging in the certainty, unchallenged, of the feast.

24–28: Lines presenting an alternative, contrasting, response to the scene : sitting, not standing; toying with flowers, in a quiet emotion like the restful peace after long tiredness...

29–33: an emotion related to the scene as imagined while still unvisited and virgin : the violets pursuing the changing year in their own way, with no reference to the human measurement of the seasons; the stream, magical and undisturbed, murmuring onward to itself...

33–37: the stream as seen, and sensed physically, with cheek placed down against a stone – one of a number of stones covered with moss, like sheep covered with fleece, partaking in the life of the scene.

38–42: He is in that abstract mood when – utterly content, and with mind adrift – one idles with whatever is to hand.

42–44: Then rises, unexpectedly violent, shatters the peace...

44–47: and rapes the virgin scene. Injured and soiled, she quietly surrenders. With these lines the sexual design of the poem is complete.

47–48 : The speaker of the opening of the poem is reintroduced, examining his record of these events for its accuracy...

48–52: in particular the record of his exit in total satisfaction from the scene – and with no mention of the gathering of nuts: asking himself if he was aware, even at the time, of a sense of suffering and injury among the trees; and of a watchfulness in the sky: the scene 'unseen by any human eye', but not unseen.

53–55: The poet turns to a virgin companion, present not at the event but at the time of the recording of the narrative, and hopes that she will learn by his experience, and enter such vulnerable places always with gentleness – gentleness of intent and, if she must touch, gentleness of touch; carefully, for there is a living presence, sensitive and watchful.

NUTTING

It seems a day,
(I speak of one from many singled out)
One of those heavenly days which cannot die,
When forth I sallied from our cottage-door,
And with a wallet o'er my shoulder slung,
A nutting crook in hand, I turned my steps
Towards the distant woods, a Figure quaint,
Tricked out in proud disguise of Beggar's weeds
Put on for the occasion, by advice
And exhortation of my frugal Dame.
Motley accoutrements! of power to smile
At thorns, and brakes, and brambles, and, in truth,
More ragged than need was. Among the woods,
And o'er the pathless rocks, I forced my way
Until, at length, I came to one dear nook
Unvisited, where not a broken bough
Drooped with its withered leaves, ungracious sign
Of devastation, but the hazels rose
Tall and erect, with milk-white clusters hung,
A virgin scene!-A little while I stood,
Breathing with such suppression of the heart
As joy delights in; and with wise restraint
Voluptuous, fearless of a rival, eyed
The banquet, or beneath the trees I sate
Among the flowers, and with the flowers I played;
A temper known to those, who, after long
And weary expectation, have been blessed
With sudden happiness beyond all hope.
Perhaps it was a bower beneath whose leaves
The violets of five seasons re-appear
And fade, unseen by any human eye,
Where fairy water-breaks do murmur on
For ever, and I saw the sparkling foam,
And with my cheek on one of those green stones
That, fleeced with moss, beneath the shady trees,
Lay round me scattered like a flock of sheep,
I heard the murmur and the murmuring sound,
In that sweet mood when pleasure loves to pay
Tribute to ease, and, of its joy secure
The heart luxuriates with indifferent things,
Wasting its kindliness on stocks and stones,
And on the vacant air. Then up I rose,
And dragged to earth both branch and bough, with crash
And merciless ravage; and the shady nook
Of hazels, and the green and mossy bower
Deformed and sullied, patiently gave up
Their quiet being: and unless I now
Confound my present feelings with the past,
Even then, when, from the bower I turned away,
Exulting, rich beyond the wealth of kings
I felt a sense of pain when I beheld
The silent trees and the intruding sky.

Then, dearest Maiden! move along these shades
In gentleness of heart with gentle hand
Touch,—for there is a Spirit in the woods.

READING 'THREE YEARS SHE GREW IN SUN AND SHOWER'

STANZA 1

Direct opening; simple rhyme and rhythm.
Lines 1–4: An infant girl, grown three years in beauty, and apparently unguarded, is marked by Nature for Its own. Nature speaks – a watchful and active presence...
4–6: that will take her and shape her into a maturity of Its own design;

STANZA 2

7–8: as her loving inspiration and guide.
9–12: Wherever she finds herself she will feel an overseeing presence, urging, restraining.

STANZA 3

13–15: She will know the world in its wildest, gaiest moods...
16–18: and at its quietest and most still; learning from both.

STANZA 4

And in the heavens likewise:
19–20: Finding nobility in the clouds. The willow tree (out of place here in the plan of the poem) will lean down to protect.
20–24: She will find in the heavens, even at their most violent, a silent grace to shape her virginal form,

STANZA 5

25–26: She will find love in creation at its most distant (in the stars) –
27–28: and at its most intimate – in hidden places, with turning small streams...
29–30: where beauty born of the stream's murmuring 'shall pass into her face' – a striking image, but not out of place among her responses as imagined by Nature; and with the physical detail clear from 'Nutting', the book's preceding poem: the murmuring of the stream sensed with cheek against a stone.

STANZA 6

31–33: The physical responses continue – more difficult to accept, with body changing in response to the extent of her joy...
34–36: although it is still Nature that is imagining and speaking. Nature reveals a human aspect; it is the human narrator naming the chosen child, the great happenings in the poem placed as thoughts in Lucy's mind for their shared future.

STANZA 7

37–39: Potential thoughts and great happenings already cancelled by the infant Lucy's death...
39–40: leaving only the peaceful scene – scene of the original 'sun and shower';
41–42: brief memory; and an emptiness of time.

'THREE YEARS SHE GREW IN SUN AND SHOWER'

Three years she grew in sun and shower;
Then Nature said, 'A lovelier flower
On earth was never sown;
This child I to myself will take;
She shall be mine, and I will make
A lady of my own.

'Myself will to my darling be
Both law and impulse: and with me
The girl, in rock and plain,
In earth and heaven, in glade and bower,
Shall feel an overseeing power
To kindle or restrain.

'She shall be sportive as the fawn
That wild with glee across the lawn
Or up the mountain springs;
And hers shall be the breathing balm,
And hers the silence and the calm
Of mute insensate things.

'The floating clouds their state shall lend
To her; for her the willow bend;
Nor shall she fail to see
Even in the motions of the storm
Grace that shall mould the maiden's form
By silent sympathy.

'The stars of midnight shall be dear
To her; and she shall lean her ear
In many a secret place
Where rivulets dance their wayward round,
And beauty born of murmuring sound
Shall pass into her face.

'And vital feelings of delight
Shall rear her form to stately height,
Her virgin bosom swell;
Such thoughts to Lucy I will give
While she and I together live
Here in this happy dell.'

Thus Nature spake. The work was done—
How soon my Lucy's race was run!
She died, and left to me
This heath, this calm, and quiet scene;
The memory of what has been,
And never more will be.

Drawing Lessons

JEFFREY WAINWRIGHT

after John Ruskin   *for Brian Maidment*

'Now if you can draw that stone,
you can draw anything'

look your stone antagonist boldly in the face

I do. I mean, I try. I falter but do not fall back.
I will valiant be! It is not my pencil,
nor my hand but the bounds of my attention
that have no membraned stuff tough enough.

How does a stone wait for us? At the ready?
Why does it antagonise so? Resistant
to all entreaty, obduring, yet what might
it relieve us of? What could it pillage?

Then why must I stand up, why try to seize
and satchel the likeness of a stone?
Is this how to live on the earth about us,
believing a stone is honoured by a line?

A stone, a leaf, their fragile shadows clinging –
we are not of them however proximate they seem.
And yet 'their fragile shadows clinging'
will adhere. How do I muster a tender act?

the best drawing-masters are the woods and hills

You are my *best drawing-masters*, you and your kin
and I am instructed. But does my pencilling
bring me towards a sight of you,
even to a glimpsing, the moon inside a cloud?

Everything is human, nothing looks itself:
the leaf is sorrow bent, the willows'
cradle-arch secures the headlong stream,
the waters either errant or stymied in their pools,

the trees clustered but still unneighbourly,
even you, old stone, junk from a hapless cliff,
are harried and beset,
made but to serve my cognisance.

O tree, stone, air, babbling brook, will you not be
yourself!
I see you sometimes strolling sometimes spry,
but only ever as you are not, captured
again and again just so, but nothing like.

dense and unmalleable this world

Dense and unmalleable this world indeed,
so what is to be done? Stories try to
hoick it into order, patting it like butter
or a brick, something to put a finger on,

a dish or a flight of consequences.
But how do they end? *vain loves and fruitless deaths*.
The pencil line at least is modest, no exhilaration,
often a *wholly grey or rainy day* is best.

In such a light tree-boughs stand like dark rivers
against the sky, the sky like long-fallen snow,
and I'm trying again at my spiny conker-shells:
can I get them to split upon the page?

Oh my scuffed, rubbed, dirtied patient page,
there seems nothing between the world and you
but in some shape it stays out there.
Is there a tender point, a tender thought to move it?

mew and howl

mew and howl how much indeed do I *mew and howl*,
not for the drudgery of shading but for the whole
codge-modge I am making –
the lines off-beam, the shadowing too

profound, the volumes pancake-flat,
and as I rub and rub and try again
the stale bread I use scratches and maims
this smudged, fingerprinted and dishonest page

and crumbles about the room. Yet I must go slow!
I know that the swish of a line drawn
with what is called freedom is wrong,
as leaving bread to waste upon a windowsill

is wrong, that I should never let my natural hand
think it might go free, that hereabouts is nothing
but itself. Better the codge-modge, I'm thinking.
I cannot be God, not even on a page.

*Nature will show you nothing if you set yourself up for her
master*

And why not, pal? How much poke does she think
she has?
Look at these naïve potato-flowers,
so silly, so virginal, they are bound to look my way,
the orange-tree, for all its spikes, cannot act

rebarbative enough. Turves, a slouching hare,
another sunless copse, fields without folk,
the charcoal tumble of a mountain stream,
a makeshift grotto in the rocks above,

my cross-hatched lilies, all these stand there,
dutiful and still, not an itch not a twitch.
For Nature has nothing new to show,
nothing unanticipated, unforeseen,

unmined and unrefined, nothing my stylus
cannot incise, nothing unbidden by guile
or charm or force. I am *set up*,
a master and bestride, and Nature moonstruck, daft.

shutting the light gradually up (i)

The faintest of lines drawn across the page
sets this process off; a bucket of pitch,
a broad brush, heavy-laden, becomes logical,
and we see the end of art is blackness.

So what now? Thankfully, some strides are easy,
especially in thought, and just one
will take us to the Half-Way House
licensed for the sale and consumption

of alcoholic beverages in some full name
always neatly legible beneath the transom
of etched or frosted glass. Inside the varnished
wood is styled in brushed horizontal strokes

and everywhere there are circles to be seen,
coins, beermats, stools, fixings of many sorts
and hues and patterns in clothes, labels, skin.
Though never untouched, light does pass.

shutting the light gradually up (ii)

Meanwhile, back at the artists' camp, the light had
changed.
Was this a 'trick', a variation of the variation
slyly declined from its routine pilgrimage?
Light holds so many options it can ignore habit,

and even though we artists exult in this
we cannot keep up – now we see it now we
see it otherwise. Loosed from the sun
light turns us without mercy or regard,

so many particulars, special cases, glimpses left aside,
that's a dry leaf scurrying not a snake or a shrew,
a tree cut off against a now truncated sky,
a weir-stone turning its water into perfect glass.

Weary of this we are, just like the mythic soul
who journeyed on in timeless and perpetual light
until she sat, closed her eyes, and *shutting the light*
gradually up, gave us the darkness and the night she
dreamed.

there's a line and a natural line

there's a line and a natural line
but what you will ask of course is how
anyone can be that definite. The line defines
is all I can say, which is convenient.

In latitudes where the sky is lineless
you can wait all day to limn a cloud edge.
Swing-ropes tautened by a broken seat
hang there as stand-ins, their twinings and plaitings

made natural by gravity you could say,
a convenience that I imagine as
stair rods, cartoon rain, lines heading straight down
something as natural as you can get.

But the bough curves upwards and the hand
strives to follow it, leaps to think that it has found
the natural line and cries out boldly:
'Look, we are as one! Me and this patient tree!'

there was a spacious half of seat vacant in my little
hooded carriage

Verticals, horizontals, diagonals, antagonists all.
A line that ought to be approaching neatly
saunters suddenly aside, takes the perspective
so the void collapses and the space is lost.

The paper neither smiles nor scowls, an ice dive
could find no mischief there however deep it is.
I could arraign the always-otherness
of natural things like the four pines across

the near-horizon, five when I look again.
Yet all the world out there demands is some attention.
Four or five? That at least. They even stand
stock still this morning as though to be of help.

Snow falls on the river and is then something else.
On some scaffolding that man in a high-vis tee
must watch his step. Better his foot does not find
a gangplank changing into vacant air.

...creatures who are every instant perishing...

...creatures who are every instant perishing...
like a waterfall: there and at the same time vanishing;
always ellipsed but always with us.
They leave me tongue-tied but never leave.

Because *what is instantly helpful to creatures*
who are every instant perishing is...
revolving this is a regular shame.
Let me be helpful, in pencilling and elsewhere.

I draw a bar tightly across a page
and set to work. To one side
I scribble and scribble to a coalhouse black
and then seek to shade stealthily

toward the other side, greyer and lighter
with every touch into the page's patient white.
Dissatisfaction with what I do is *wholesome*, but I might
graduate to show some creature in the twilit sky.

the best answerer of questions is perseverance

The beauty of the light needs not to be
attested to, it boils and shudders anyway,
so to see things in themselves is to possess
composition enough – that can be securely said.

But then the gusts of sunlight unman me,
even as I lift my eyes to meet it
line and mass dissolve again just as I
duck down beneath the parapet.

To be so lost in it, feeling blind,
no more than scrabbling as though this world
were lightless and once more the pencil blunts,
breaks and even the page begins to snigger.

The best answerer of questions is perseverance.
That will not be of the saintly kind
but that through wind and weather, all I am allowed
to help me seek whatever waits inside the light.

it would be bad advice that made you bold

But what scares me is to be thought
pusillanimous – 'Da da dee da da!
What yer waiting for Wainy?'
and meanwhile here comes Big Ballsy

pounding down the slope, going hard for it,
the big doffer, up and over the brook and –
nearly makes it, he falls back on landing,
you can see he's wet through to his pants.

But he dunna care, he beats his chest, he's ready
for the Cabaret Voltaire and grabs a megaphone:
DOFFERCOCKSTERBROCKSTERDOO –
surely this is 'the language of Paradise'!

But Ballsy had gone about as fer as he could go
and took up his pen again. 'I never could bid
chaos welcome', he wrote, and I am daunted anew.
Labour on therefore courageously.

You will never love art well till you love what she mirrors better

...what she mirrors better. Is shadowing then
what she is about, and why we are so enamoured,
so very smit by colour and by sock wool
figured from a herring's useful skeleton?

Perhaps, but this makes me drawn to devilry.
R's modest 'what' is of course venerable
Ma Nature, our mother even when she was only
glops, molt and flame, not the jovial dame

of ladysmock, author of zephyrs and the noble nod
of cedar, oak and lime, who preceded
and must take precedence, making us feel small
as even pismires are revealed as better organised.

This is not how I choose to be chastised.
When I seek the shadow what looks back is human,
as mutable as a leaf or the artist's eye,
which looks and then makes up what she sees.

Again Like a Dream

William Empson's *The Face of the Buddha* *

MARK THOMPSON

WILLIAM EMPSON'S AFFINITY for Buddhism was well known; references are scattered through *Some Versions of Pastoral*, written in Japan (1931–34) while he was also working on *The Face of the Buddha*, and his version of the 'Fire Sermon' stands like an obsidian monument at the front of his Collected Poems: 'When he is weary of these things, he becomes empty of desire. When he is empty of desire, he becomes free. When he is free he knows that he is free [...]'

In September 1944, Empson asked his publisher to consider 'a little book about Far Eastern Buddhist sculpture' with many photographs and only ten thousand words, unless 'you want more'. Chatto & Windus was cool. Empson said he would try elsewhere. If he did, it was without success; before he took his wife and children to Beijing in 1947, he entrusted the typescript (grown, we now know, to thirty thousand words) to his old friend John Davenport. Davenport gave it to the poet and editor Tambimuttu, who later passed it to a fourth party, Richard March. Davenport meanwhile, raddled by alcohol, forgot what he had done and eventually confessed that he left it in a taxi. Empson bore the blow nobly. The lost work passed into legend. Jacob Empson recalls that his father 'often talked about *The Face of the Buddha*'. Rewriting it, however, was out of the question 'as of course all the illustrations were lost'. Then, a decade ago, it turned up among March's papers in the British Library.

Even unseen, *The Face of the Buddha* was known to be unique in Empson's career, both as a departure from literature and as measuring an immersion in Buddhist culture and history deeper than anything promised by those hints. This made it unimaginable. Yet here, wonderfully, it is – a new book by the best English critic of the last century.

What, then, has been recovered? In the first place, a 'brief survey of the sculpture of the Buddha and Buddhist personages', with new colour plates added to the author's seventy-four monochrome images, and a pretty hand-drawn map of 'Empson's Asia' on the endpapers; then, an original theory about asymmetry in the faces of certain sculptures; and lastly, brief reflections on the moral essence of Buddhism. The survey begins with remarks on 'The Type in General'. From the first page, *The Face of the Buddha* shows Empson at full imaginative stretch, his incomparable best:

The drooping eyelids of the great creatures are heavy with patience and suffering, and the subtle irony which offends us in their raised eyebrows (it is quite a common expression among Europeans, though curiously avoided in our portraits) is in effect an appeal to us to feel, as they do, that it is odd that we let our desires subject us to so much torment in the world.

Read it again for the music (*adagio assai*), the exactness of 'offends', the parenthetical glance homeward, the solicitude ascribed to stone or bronze, the humour of 'odd', always one of Empson's cardinal epithets. While the writing rises often to such height, *The Face* is not an extended prose-poem. It has work to do, compacting observation and research, testing impressions against evidence, explaining, puzzling over problems. As ever, Empson's style has an ideal sociability, never talking down, moving with the motion of living thought, yet self-communing. It is exhilarating to be treated so civilly as brighter than we are. The book retains the open-collared and wholly unpretentious air of a sport, and hums with the excitement of investigation; yet the seriousness of the undertaking is not disguised (though neither is it openly avowed). Partha Mitter's wise preface speaks of a spiritual quest.

The writing about particular sculptures ranks with the best of *Seven Types of Ambiguity* (1930) and *Some Versions* (1935). Yet the objects of his attention are made in a medium other than his own. His interpretations of sculpture are simpler than his literary analyses because there are no other words for Empson to get in amongst with words of his own. After seeing him at an Aldermaston march, Alan Brownjohn wrote a poem about the middle-aged Empson's 'fierce empirical gaze'. There is a lot of empirical gazing in this book, and it catches things we would miss (those raised eyebrows), but any fierceness implied by such scrutiny is dispelled by the pleasure conveyed. Here he is in Seoul, facing a sixth-century bronze Maitreya (a successor to the Gautama Buddha):

> The hands have a remarkable quality which also reappears in early Japanese work; they seem at first mere cylinders bent crudely with tweezers when hot enough to be soft, but you begin to imagine what it would feel like to have those hands, and realise that if you saw them in a living creature it would affect you as divine. Maybe the fact that the fingers are equally thick all the way down is what keeps them from oversoftness. The eternity of the calm is contrasted with the carelessness with which the pose has been adopted for a moment; the universe is holding its breath till the coming Buddha completes the movement of its right hand and opens its eyes.

The beautiful contrast echoes the closing words of Empson's preface to the 1947 edition of *Seven Types*: 'so straddling a commotion and so broad a calm'. And here, thoughtfully enraptured at Bayon, near Angkor:

> Cambodia is the only part of the world which made a success of colossal heads as a unit of architecture. The term colossal is often used for anything larger than lifesize, but here it is meant seriously: the heads carved in relief on the towers of the Bayon are six feet high. Very big heads were tried fairly often in Buddhist art up to a late date (Burma, northern China and Japan have the main surviving ones) but they are all as dead as mutton. The Khmer effect of being completely withdrawn into a dream and yet dreaming with great activity and pleasure, is for some reason compatible with great size. [...] It is constructed on an orderly foursquare plan with turrets rising in tiers, each big enough to hold one of the heads on each side; there are platforms going round them at several levels, and more of the heads on the central tower. Thus you can get right in among these monsters and see them from all angles at once, with a bewildering repetition, again like a dream in that ordinary perspective seems to be suspended. [...] I hope that they stood for the Boddhisattva of Mercy even if identified with the reigning king (as is now generally believed); if they stood for Shiva in his aspect of lust and destruction the nightmare intended must have been a terrible one. But I was unable to shake off the idea of absolute protection and understanding which is the direct impression given by the stone.

The mix of 'direct impression' with rapid reasoning, as if extemporised, carries through the knottier specialised passages of the survey. A chapter about expressions on the statues appraises noses, brows, eyebrows, eyelids, lips, smiles – components of 'the human facial machinery' as well as hands and drapery, proposing categories and interpretive distinctions with finesse and humour. A Japanese wooden figure is 'straining his mouth when depicted into a smile of thin-lipped sensual embarrassment; it makes him look constipated in his determination; the will to destroy will has so far failed to destroy itself, and he is sitting there trying.' When expression fails, Empson is brusque; a 'huge Buddha' in Korea is no better than 'a great slug'.

This all builds up to Empson's theory that many of the finest heads show an intention to 'make the face more human' by making 'the two sides of the head different'. This lets them combine 'things that seem incompatible, especially a complete repose or detachment with an active power to help the worshipper'. Not all the statues he likes have asymmetrical faces, nor was 'the trick' practised everywhere (India is excluded). 'But I think the method was used often, and that it is a main source of the wonderful variety which the Far Eastern artists achieved within the formula of the Buddha facial type.' Broadly, the right side 'shows what the person has accomplished, the left his congenital equipment or inheritance.' Hence his interpretation of the Kudara Kannnon (the Boddhisattva or 'saint' associated with compassion) at Nara in Japan, carved from camphor wood:

> The puzzlement and the good humour of the face are all on the left, also the maternity and the rueful but amiable smile. The right is the divinity; a birdlike innocence and wakefulness; unchanging in irony, unresting in good works; not interested in humanity or for that matter in itself.

And hence too his gloss on Karsh's wartime photograph of Churchill: the 'administrator on the right [...] and on the left the petulance, the rancour, the romanticism, the gloomy moral strength and the range of imaginative power.'

Seeking corroboration, Empson cites 'some recent psychologists' who in the 1930s had published theories about facial asymmetry, and then cannot resist turning their definitions inside out ('both formulations are very slippery'). Better to his purpose, he cuts up photographs of asymmetrical heads; the right-right and left-left composites seem to show different sculptures entirely. Empson is convinced that consistent and successful effects could not have been obtained across such a swathe of the globe unintentionally, without a theory, and he waves away the objection that 'simple masons' would not be capable of techniques to express religious ideas: 'I do not understand why a man troubles to become an expert on these things if he thinks they were made by dolts. Sculptors were important enough to be specially imported.'

The ascription and defence of intention cue the last chapter, where Empson tackles a Western prejudice that Buddhism is a 'passive, pessimistic and indeed reactionary creed'. On the contrary, 'It has been a civilising force in wide areas of the world, and there is nothing less reactionary than the idea that "all this misery is unnecessary: if you renounce selfishness you can free yourself from your chains."' Empson sees the supreme quality of Japanese sculptures as proof that the 'strength of Buddhism as a civilising agent was never more impressive than at the end of its journey across Asia'. After disputing Sir Charles Eliot's view on Buddhist pessimism, he lightly airs the critical and ethical principle that pleasure is the index of morality.

> On the fundamental issues I have nothing more profound to say than that it takes all sorts to make a world. But it is true I think that a desire and competence to do practical good must somehow be felt in the religion whenever the art which it inspires is deeply enjoyed. It may be some failure to insist on this aspect of its doctrine that made Buddhism fall so regularly into weakness and partial corruption [...] there seems no reason to doubt that the religion was doing practical good during the periods when the art feels as if it was doing so.

Critics should trust their intuitions ahead of their judgement, then test them against the evidence; historians too, perhaps. Empson's mission to understand Buddhist sculptures begins with delight in their presence. In an important sense, it also ends there; delight is his touchstone; he wants to account for it but not to move beyond it. 'I have been treating the statues as people', he concludes disarmingly, 'and trying to describe their personalities. But Buddhism does not believe in a personality.' This forthrightness is typical, and so is the adjudication: 'It would be an odd, but not an unreasonable, thing if the profoundest studies of character in all sculptures have proceeded from a painstaking application in detail of the doctrine that there is no such thing as a character at all.' This cryptic finding reflects Empson's settled view that the highest religious art should be expected to outrun the tenets that inspired it.

The editor, Rupert Arrowsmith, asked several present-day scholars to comment on Empson's theory. One expressed 'full agreement'; another had never noticed asymmetries and attached no significance to them; the other two felt that asymmetry must be 'accidental when it occurs' because there is 'no religious textual basis or tradition in belief or practice' for it. Scholars should be prudent, but the lack of curiosity here is dismal. Arrowsmith might have pressed his scholars harder, and might also have picked up Empson's complex supposition about Buddhism 'doing practical good' in periods of highest artistic creativity, reporting the evidence either way. Perhaps the 'period feel' of the book – attractive in itself – deterred him. It was right to involve a Buddhist in this project, but John Haffenden should also have been engaged. As Empson's biographer and peerless editor, he would trace the book's filaments of contact with his words and thought. Arrowsmith rightly mentions the essay on 'Double Plots' from *Some Versions* (though the play in question is *Henry IV*, not *Henry V*). Empson's praise of Shakespeare's mix of comic and serious scenes for giving 'an impression of dealing with life completely' is indeed like his praise of asymmetry. This is only one of many echoes between *The Face of the Buddha* and *Some Versions*, however, and more should also be said of the relation between asymmetry and ambiguity.

The book alters our sense of Empson's canon. It turns out that *Milton's God* (1961) was Empson's second study of how religious art challenges and enlarges the doctrine which belief entails. His conclusions about the moral qualities of Buddhism and Christianity are of course antithetical; this makes another connection. *Milton's God* examines the poet's impulse to humanise its remote non-human entities; it elaborates and extends the essay about Milton and Bentley in *Some Versions*, which dwells upon 'the person Satan'. His detection of humanising impulses among the anonymous sculptors in East Asia anticipates his attribution to Milton (or a part of his imagination) of humane resistance to the cruelty of Christian doctrine. He even repeated the broad structure of the earlier book, working up to a final chapter about the religion.

Arrowsmith is at his best in his account of Empson's travels in search of Buddhist sculpture. When he visited Hase Dera temple to see Japan's largest sculpture in wood, in 1933, 'the immense carving was still lit for the visitor by the traditional method, which involved a monk hoisting a pair of lanterns on a rope in stages up the sculpture's façade, so that only one section of it became visible at a time.' As he watched the gradual disclosure of the eleven-headed Bodhisattva, nine metres tall and gilded, did Empson recall his poem 'Letter II', written at Cambridge and given to Desmond Lee, object of a reticent passion ('a tumult never to be told') – '*Searching the cave gallery of your face / My torch meets fresco after fresco ravishes / Rebegets me* [...]'? Was this coincidence in his mind when he wrote later that year that poets 'tend to make in their lives a situation they have already written about'? We cannot know, but it is fair to wonder whether Empson's enchantment by images of Buddhist renunciation signalled a need or even a will to gain distance from tormenting desires.

Unthinkable that Empson would broach such matters in print, here or anywhere; 'I am not at all secretive', he once told a correspondent; nor was he at all confessional. He might, though, have made a travel book about his visits to temples. Moving around Asia was arduous as well as picturesque; Empson was witty and observant in letters to friends

('Always rather embarrassing to wonder what one gets out of travel to make up for its privations; except that it requires so much imagination to stay at home'). When his publisher suggested a travel book about China, in 1938, he mulled over the idea but could not talk himself into it. ('What worries me is to know whether a chat book would be bad for the reputation, but in fact it obviously wouldn't if done in a quiet casual way.') Travel writing simply lacked, in his eye, the merit of sufficient value. 'The truth is that ill-natured jokes about your companions are very nearly all you think of while travelling, so naturally that has to be the material.' Material for gossip, then, not for print ('Quennell wrote a good book about his and my job [*A Superficial Journey through Tokyo and Peking*] though he oughtn't to have done it').

Instead we have instants of travel: Empson's waking dream at Bayon, and aesthetic bliss in Piccadilly. A ceramic figure of a *luohan* (Buddhist saint) seen at the Royal Academy in 1935 'seemed to me so much alive that it turned the people looking at it in the London Exhibition into twittering ghosts'. This phrase – not to be confused with 'ghost Twittering' – did not feature in his *Listener* article about Buddha sculptures in February 1936. I think it came to mind when he was rewriting in the mid 1940s, and its source was Eliot's *Burnt Norton*, which he would have read on publication in April 1936 (the month after the exhibition closed). He was extraordinarily susceptible to Eliot's influence ('I do not know for certain how much of my own mind he invented'), and the vision of 'strained time-ridden faces / Distracted from distraction by distraction' in London, ending 'Not here the darkness in this twittering world' would easily associate itself with his memory of the mute figure in Piccadilly. The phrase recurs twice in his journalism over the year following Eliot's death in January 1965, when he was also in touch with Davenport; perhaps this communication stirred a muscle-memory of the lost book.

What Leavis said of Empson's first book holds true for *The Face of the Buddha*, which should have been his third: it shows a mind alive 'to the exciting strangeness of the present phase of human history'. This may sound paradoxical for a book about ancient sculpture, yet the 1930s saw remarkable writing by young men who had been schoolboys during the Great War and as adults were avid for new cultural horizons. Inspired by Ezra Pound and psychoanalysis, Adrian Stokes (born 1902) elicited an aesthetic morality from carved marble panels in an Italian town, extolling in *Stones of Rimini* (1934) techniques that let stone 'come to life'. Robert Byron (born 1905) was impelled by a theorising love of medieval Persian architecture to make his way to Afghanistan; *The Road to Oxiana* (1937) merges gossip, thrills and meditation, a gorgeous style with the seeming spontaneity of a journal.

Borges held that every good book has its counter-book. *The Road to Oxiana* and *The Face of the Buddha* play this role for each other. 'The Gumbad-i-Kabus ranks with the great buildings of the world', Byron pronounced, as Empson commended the statues of Nara for 'their freedom, tenderness, and power and the universality which makes them citizens of the high art of the world.' Amateurs in their respective niches, gentleman eccentrics somehow immune against serious mishap, they sought perspectives from which to look westwards more accurately. Byron saw 'modern nationalism' spreading its poison from Europe to Persia and as far as the Oxus. Empson felt Japanese jingoism 'like a weight on the back of the neck'. Both wanted to strengthen the general immunity against nationalism: cultural or spiritual remedies for political disorder, hence bound to fail in the near run; stoicism was part of the project. Neither man found comfort in communism; 'reactionary' in one of the quotations above is a reminder that while Empson was pursuing Buddha sculptures, many of his contemporaries chased a different enlightenment, thirsting for the red dawn over Europe. 'Somebody must trespass on the taboos of modern nationalism,' wrote defiant Byron in April 1934, 'in the interests of human reason. Business can't. Diplomacy won't. It has to be people like us.'

Yet the differences too are salient. Reaching Bamian in Afghanistan, Byron was repelled by the giant Buddhas: 'it is their negation of sense, the lack of any pride in their monstrous flaccid bulk.' Empson too wrote crossly about displeasing sculptures (that Korean slug), but Byron then generalised: an 'air of repose, graceful but empty' is 'the best one can expect of Buddhist iconography.' Empson shows what a shallow dash was cut here. On the other hand, when his attention is caught by architecture, Byron unfurls descriptions that are lavish, evocative and meticulous. Empson is laconic, almost casual by comparison; he wants us to focus on what most matters. Each is generous to the reader in his own way, incompatible with the other's.

Byron beguiles by entertaining; his book is a performance, brilliant, choleric and entranced, condescending and lyrical. Among the targets of his malice is the appetite of Western tourists for the oriental exotic. Yet he too supplies this commodity in his elegant way: 'At Ismailabad I sat under a tree on a patch of emerald grass strewn with ox bones, and ate a bowl of curds'. 'The car smelt of roses as we crossed the frontier into Turkestan.' Local colour and vivid temperament interweave in his tapestried narrative. He remains consciously the maverick Englishman abroad, a peculiar credit to the nation that he enjoys deploring. Empson's Englishness is not performed; it shows in his language and absorption in his task. The human type is scientific rather than aesthetic. He is motivated by pleasure in his apprehension of the universal meaning of the statues, not in the spectacle of his experience of them, or in the statues' sheer remoteness. If remoteness mattered, it was in the sense of Buddhist distance from the turmoil of attachment ('The drooping eyelids of the great creatures are heavy with patience and suffering'). There is not a malicious word in the book. As for local colour, Empson's statues might almost have been scattered around Belgium. So the unwritten travel book is no loss, for in its stead we have something unique, evidence of what Empson would come to call and to call for, against the paranoid nationalism fostered by the Cold War, 'world-mindedness'. A graver threat in our time to this virtue is posed by economic globalisation and its forces – a paradox that Empson would have no trouble unpicking.

The reason he could not write *The Face of the Buddha* again was not the illustrations; images are replaceable. The older Empson was distracted with crusades and crotchets, denouncing the Christian God as 'the wickedest thing yet invented by the black heart of man' (this in the year of Eichmann's trial and the Berlin Wall) and dismayingly obsessed with 'libels' inflicted by other critics on favourite writers. We are wards to time, which leaves no thing intact. Damaged by a lifetime's heavy drinking, he could no more have recreated this marvellously open-minded, open-spirited account than he could have started to write poems again. Give homage to Jamie Andrews for unearthing it at the British Library (a haunt of Empson's early and late), and thanks to Rupert Arrowsmith and Oxford University Press for polishing the facets.

* William Empson, *The Face of the Buddha*, edited by Rupert Arrowsmith (Oxford University Press, 2016), 152 pages, £30.

'The Cabin Boy' & Other Poems

GABRIELLA ATTEMS

The Cabin Boy

Now was November, the days spooked
with sea light. On board the Sylvan he thought
of the coppices back home, of the gusts dragging
leaves around the spinney. Too poor to have him

learn a useful trade like shoe- or wheel-making,
they'd been sad to see him go. But hadn't he
taken to this like a clam to water, his knees
flexing with the surge and pull on the towering,

plunging castle that was the three-master. There
was something familiar in the song that crept
into his sleep, something the wind had brought
to him in the rustling of leaves, something

he'd overheard in the landing of geese, like
a rumour of salt and distance in their feathers.
He was near the trapdoor when it happened,
a smell of gold ripe sun rising from the hull:

sudden and unexpected a gale and the vessel
veered, came rocks, the cold Atlantic seepage.

People say it's the local fisherman who found
him, but wasn't there a woman in her ruined shawl
on the shingle for dillisk and limpets the storm
had thrown up who sensed a change around

the island and sent out Jack. Three days
on the Sovereign's naked rock and how the salt
had whipped his face, shrivelled his hands,
and him only a gaunt youth of twelve, maybe

thirteen. Too late for his crew. Bodies
were buried in Kinure, unmarked graves here
and there in Páirc a' Tempaill, as if orderliness
was only wasted on the dead; much later

came a plaque to remember them, the Sylvan's
downcome and its only survivor, the cabin boy.

The Stationary Whale

Stillness is his talent, poised and silent
inside the cove, while all around him, flux
is every ocean creature's rise and fall. So
the current feeds him crustaceans with dillisk
and sea salad all day until the tide recedes
and he's laid in the open a while – he doesn't mind –
showing the sun his back, his skin a slate-black
so smooth silence slips off it and becomes
that space between waves. Sea birds and geese
come to land on his head and human animals
bend over his side to study the barnacles that map
suns so strange as though they were picked
from old galaxies, trajectories he covers
in his dreams that resemble waking, an expanse
as vast as his age is ageless. Sometimes
the sky is a weight of gushing rain that breaks
into heather-light at dusk above the cove.
You can see he's hungry for the world
carrying all these suns on his belly. He treks
miles inside the kelp forest, her palmed
leaves waving at him like an old friend.
He hasn't bothered practising his
echolocation enough for it to work well
in the aeons since his tectonic making,
time to him is but a glassy windless surge.
They say, he weighs a couple more stones –
or rather boulders – than his cousins out
at sea. Still his arteries are not as wide
as a Blue's, not quite big enough for you
or me to swim through, but vibrant and
pulsing with song. He likes the clicking
noise people make with small black devices,
when in the storm his blow is best seen
and flowers over the outcrop; he never gets
to see it arrested on photo paper, the card
grainy and matt like green sandstone
or like sea mist that blurs the horizon-line
and renders the elements of sea and sky
almost alike if it wasn't for the look
in his eye that is no mystery to the ocean.

Eclipse

'Prisonniers des gouttes d'eau,
nous ne sommes que des animaux perpétuels.'
André Breton & Philippe Soupault

The moon thinks it's a gift,
pushes its weight
into our marrow, a halter

on the daylight's neck. What
does it do to the swell,
rising a sudden surge of fish, silvery

but finless.
Does the Danube heave
at one end, and empty out

her straights on mud flats,
her giants captive in their age-old
sturgeon body, unable

to moult or take to the land
while eels are hugging
the slime? A child in the park,

a girl in white shoes, dreams
she walks between two
fields, her aunties are foxgloves

shaking with laughter
and she turns to the sky, questioning
its mauve powder – how

it seems ready to fall apart.
More than pollen, damp
like dregs of wine, thickening

the streets, smudging
sidewalks and housefronts – this
is a long moan of light. Then

as sudden as the undefeated racehorse
would release its tendons and
erupt from the starting gate,

the sun pushes,
pushes and gives birth
to her own light again.

Later Emperors

Evan Jones

1. Philip the Arab

When Gordian III asked to remain emperor,
the army booed and hissed.
So he offered to share his power
and the army clanked their spears.
He consented to the rank of Caesar.
But the army refused him.
Could he act then as prefect?
No. They declined outright.
Finally he pleaded for his life.
Philip the Arab, silent till that moment,
considered letting him live.
He thought of Gordian's innocence,
the sympathy the innocent engender,
the riots that sympathy sets in motion,
the half-finished, the order
he was about to give.

2. Valerian

Yes, yes, the Persian monarch Sapor,
mounting his horse, said to
his allies – they who feared the armies
of Rome – as he steadied his right foot
on Valerian's neck and looked
up through the stars.

3. Zenobia

All that remains of Zenobia's past life
is in ruins: her reign, her studies
of art and literature and history,
the great minds who informed her thinking
when Palmyra took the world stage.
On trial before the Emperor Aurelian,
she lost her nerve, and implicated, amid others,
the sublime Longinus in crimes
against Rome. He was put to death.
And Zenobia? Sometimes not even
death will leave us sure of an ending.

4. Probus

In the market, Probus
stopped to sample a bit
of cheese, a bit of fish,
and then continued walking
towards the circus, where he'd
ordered transplanted a forest
of five thousand trees filled
with a thousand ostrich,
a thousand stag,
a thousand fallow deer,
a thousand wild boar.

Tomorrow he would
massacre one hundred
lions and lionesses, two
hundred leopards and three
hundred bears. For today,
cheese and fish were enough
to mask the smell.

5. Carus, Struck by Lightning AD 283

Aged, feeble Carus during
the stormy night called for his mother,
droned, reeled, balked, barked
at the tent poles and servants.
Feverish now, when young he was a tent
pole, a severe and simple man,
as Gibbon wrote, a soldier,
satisfied with stale bacon
and stone-hard peas. He passed.
We set the imperial pavilion
on fire, suggested it was lightning,
an act of god. Wrong,
I know, though not exactly wrong.

6. Diocletian

Diocletian, having resigned the world,
died where he was born.
For his last nine years he planted
cabbage with his own hands
at Salona. The arts he said to friends,
often, over dinner, are equally difficult,
but reigning is the most difficult art.
We might like to disagree
but he lived in an era
when the poets kept silent.

'The Starfish' & Other Poems

Isabel Galleymore

The Starfish

creeps like expired meat –
fizzy-skinned, pentamerously-legged,
her underfur of sucking feet
shiver upon an immobile mussel
whose navy mackintosh is zipped
against the anchor of this fat paw,
this seemingly soft nutcracker who exerts
such pressure until the mussel's jaw
drops a single millimetre. Into this cleft
she'll press the shopping bag of her stomach
and turn the mollusc into broth,
haul in the goods and stumble off,
leaving a vacant cubicle,
a prayer come apart.

The Slipper Limpet

In the double-dark of the sea at night,
in a shoe of shell, a stomach-foot
with a growing appetite
invites a dozen to generate
a vertical queue, a carefully organised high-rise
orgy with her, its founding member,
its queen sticking to the ocean bedrock
as smaller, younger males shuffle on top
and when she's tired of the day-in day-out
rut, when her gills have breathed their last,
her nearest male inherits her sex –
two moons and he's bequeathed
her duct – and yet he'll remain stuck on her
empty bone slipper, departed Cinderella.

The Barnacles

Think of them now – Invincible, Endeavour,
well-endowed with this swamping thatch
of teeth, this citadel of calciferic bedsits
their single occupants can never leave –
what is it about November that washes
urge into this one's sinus-heart
eliciting his wily pipette
that with its several accordion folds
stretches beyond his stuck-fast self
to become a proboscis, a blind man's stick
abristle with sniffing as it wavers and knocks
against his lady neighbour's operculum doors
only to break off like part of the rigging
when the mood no longer takes him.

The Crab

Sublittoral place in which this crab sits
like the lid of a pie, its crimped edge
rests upon a mixture of pincers, legs –
two black dactyls that headline the others
dressed in the fizz and stubble of brick.
It's these bone clothes the crab outgrows
the way song, lifting a decibel, bursts
a glass; there's some civil upheaval
that allows the crab to break open
and quickly reverse out from itself –
a faded, vulnerable replica,
a soft ball of milk with milk's film skin
searching for a stone to hide beneath
for the time it takes to scab over.

Choosing

from eight million differently constructed hearts –
I couldn't – I choose to love them all:

the squid's triptych of pumps,
the snake inside its cardial sac, growing as it eats.

To say nothing will come between us,
to stay benignly intimate was –

sometimes not calling was easier,
sometimes I'd forget to touch you
and you, and you – a natural phenomenon

'dwindling' – one of a dozen breakups
from the world each day –

like the others it seemed you'd just popped out
for a pint of milk and now
nothing's conjured hearing your name.

Two Poems

MARY NOONAN

Flânerie of the Beaver

for Eugène Savitskaya

The poet walks the city brandishing the breast-
bone of a magpie, his wishbone, mark
of his poverty. He follows the ancient runnels
of the Bièvre, a river forced under the cobbles
of the Latin Quarter centuries ago.

He is tracing the tracks of the beavers
who once gnawed the bark of chestnut trees
on the river bank. He wants to be a beaver,
to shake off his man's carcass. As he walks,
he meditates on his foot, how crucial it is

to his survival, and dreams of growing his coccyx
into a tail, or releasing precious castoreum
from the glands in the castor sac behind his
testicles. If he has money, he stops for red wine
on rue Mouffetard, at 'The Glass with One Foot'.

Beavers use their musky secretion to scent their terrain.
This is his territory now, and he sniffs as he walks
the lanes to the bench behind the St Médard Church,
stretches his ears to hear the creaking of the tombs in
the old cemetery. What he hears is the howling

of the convulsing women who contorted themselves
there in the seventeenth century, working themselves
into states of mystical ecstasy at the grave of a famous
ascetic, the deacon François de Pâris. He can hear
their moans as they offer their pear/fig/melon-

shaped breasts to the young Jansenist priests.
Their resting place later passed into the hands of
a locksmith, who sold the collarbones
of the convulsionists as treasure. The poet
sits and listens to the chorus of crying tombs

wailing women and neighbourhood cats, then
walks on to the Arena of Lutèce, the Roman
gladiatorial circus of Paris. In the circle of blood,
now covered in sand, he chooses his spot, where
he places two blocks of wood, dons his hessian pants

a woollen cap and his reading glasses, then flips
his body upside-down, his head between the two
blocks, his legs perpendicular in the air.
In this posture, he reads aloud from a lengthy work.
His gentle voice booms round the amphitheatre

and pages, once read, are thrown to the wind.
Having vomited his verse, he flops to the sand
and lies there for some time, muttering *Et je ne
suis pas fatigué, et je ne suis pas fatigué*, before
gathering the pages with the help of circling children.

He walks on further, to the river, the site of the old
Gobelins tapestry workshops. He fancies he can
smell the foul effluent from the tanneries that
once lined the riverbank. The poet locates
his favourite chestnut tree, sits there

dreaming of the long incisors he will grow,
of how he will learn to bite off his testicles
when threatened by hunters, fling them in their
faces, and of how he will preen his lustrous pelt
in the sun. He wonders if he will have any memory

of the man he was: that he was innocent, that he
had tried to craft strong paper boats, float them
on the Bièvre, that he had ended carrying
the breastbone of a magpie around Paris, and that
like you today, mortal on this earth, he had a face

marked by the lines of laughter, the crevices
of pain, the face of a man or a woman, who now
has the face of a beaver, a reed between its teeth.

Elysian*

Through green, I view the city's remains. Green
glass of this colossal tower, relic of the Tiger years
whose sole lodger is me, riding the crystal warship
high above what used to be the skyline, now
the water line. Pea-green from pole to pole.

I spy with my little eye three green copper cupolas,
the crowns of City Hall, St Francis and the Courthouse
floating on moss-green clouds. A golden flying fish,
the city's flag, is still intact. I crouch above algal infinity,
a hawk plotting the horizon in vectors.

But my vantage is not safe. Bodies float by. Debris
of green cranes. At first, the floor show was all
uprooted trees, and cars. Then came the stampede.
Murders, cullings. I helped to fling the dead from
the penthouse balconies. Now I lie alone on cool marble.

The emerald light of evening floods the empty rooms,
long redundant. I listen for sounds, whirring of a lift
in the shaft, the whoosh of automatic doors.
Ghost lift, ghost doors. When I sleep, I go back
to the old city –

the mysteries of the timber yard on Water Street
where my father worked; the temptations of the sidings
of the West Cork Railway on Albert Quay; the olive
majolica tiles of the Eglinton Street Swimming Baths,
bobbing before chlorine-pricked eyes;

our flat on Lower Road, where water rats danced
over our beds as we slept. My sister and I would play
at skipping on the docks, watching for the timber boats
coming up the river from Sweden, the banana boats
gliding in from Africa, or Jamaica. And we would wait

for hours in the rain to snatch our prize: rotting bananas
flung to us by the black sailors. That was our playground,
the port where Dutch merchants built their watery empire,
a market where Bordeaux wine was swapped for butter.
I close my eyes, try to conjure butter,

the faces of my father and my sister. Fields of flowers.
Elysian fields, where the gods went to die.

* The Elysian Tower, a block of luxury apartments built in an old part of Cork city at the end of the so-called 'Celtic Tiger years'.

Biographia Literaria

DAVID WHEATLEY

Being a straight man gave Alfie plenty
of issues to work through in his poems.
The first praise Bethany got meant
that bit more coming from me. Only
at the launch did Cathal notice his name
had been misspelled on the cover.
It's not a competition, Declan told
Eveline. You've won your first competition,
Eveline congratulated Declan.
This next poem's for my enormous cock
of an ex-husband, Freya would announce
to nervous giggles. Everyone loved George
and now he's remembered only for that one line.
Thinking of slipping into the river
Harry – typical Harry – still purchased
a parking permit. Ian proved
an enthusiastic reviewer of his peers.
Prize-win by prize-win, the world
finished Jack off. Two book dedications
have just been informed Kate and Leo
are no longer together. On balance,
Mo's fling with his editor worked out
just fine. Niamh recently published
her keenly-awaited seventh collection,
perhaps her finest to date. Freezing at
the microphone, Oliver walked offstage
and never came back. Not another
honorary degree, groaned Phyllis.
I reject the heteronormative, gendered
lyric, said Queenie to great acclaim.
You wouldn't believe how feminist I am,
said Richard. Slowly Sarah got used
to being the only non-white face in the room.
Your student days at Trinity were important
to you, weren't they, interviewers would ask
Tara. These days, I find, all I care about
is the quality of light on the kitchen wall,
said Una. I can still change, said Victor.
I have someone who handles all that
for me, said Will. We tried to help
Xander but in the end there was nothing
we could do. Yolanda still pops up
on my feed now and then. Zoe died young.

The Book That Ate Itself

Travels in Surrealist New Zealand & Some Remarks on Surrealist Poetry in Britain

GREGORY O'BRIEN

THE DROWNED PAGES, 1985

Rowing an aluminium dinghy out onto Auckland's Waitemata Harbour, I was heading for Brown's Island, a.k.a Motukorea – a whale-shaped volcano, two kilometres offshore. Stashed atop a bundle of provisions near the prow was a recently acquired copy of the 1978 Penguin anthology *English and American Surrealist Poetry*, edited by Edward B. Germain – my designated reading for the day's outing. Mid-voyage, the wake of a passing ferry struck the dinghy and, along with a few other items, the Penguin went hurtling into the choppy harbour. After some flapping about, I managed to recover the book on the end of one wooden oar and deposited it back inside the dinghy. There it remained for the rest of the day, a drowned creature, bulging grotesquely with salt water. I considered abandoning it, but the wretched anthology had cost me three dollars (a princely sum at the time) so I committed to its salvage and, as far as it might go, restoration.

Back home, I put the book on top of the refrigerator, only to discover, after a few days, that the mass of weeping paper-pulp had stuck to the enamel surface; I had to tear the back cover to free it. From then on, the anthology remained open, pages facing downwards, in a dish on top of the fridge. The paper, I soon discovered, had become permanently puckered and stained a dark brown. I suspected the book might be rotting, but pressed on regardless. Within a few days, as the drying progressed, I noticed small tunnel-like holes appearing in the pages. In a manner that struck me as entirely appropriate for a Surrealist anthology, the book seemed to be eating itself.

Some obscure creature of the sea, maybe a tube-worm or parasitical slug – or, more likely, a small colony of such things – must have lodged itself inside the book during its brief oceanic submersion. As it dried out, these creatures (which I never sighted) burrowed through the pages in search of moister territories, leaving a pristine tunnel-system behind them.

I can only assume that when the book had dried out completely, the creature(s) gave up the ghost. There was a lingering whiff of *something* – maybe the book's spine had become a mausoleum of expended sea-life? Luckily, most of the tunnelling had been confined to the margins (maybe the creatures didn't like ink?) so the book's contents remained readable.

Thirty years later, it is Germain's anthology I toss onto the back seat of the car, deeming it a suitable companion for the 2013 Carcanet anthology of British Surrealist Poetry, *On the Thirteenth Stroke of Midnight*, edited by Michel Remy. I am driving north to the province of Taranaki, where an imposing museum devoted to a colourful member of the British Surrealist group, Len Lye (1901–80), opened a few months ago to a great and ongoing fanfare.

AT THE CENTRE OF LEN LYE

The Len Lye Centre, New Plymouth, New Zealand

Located in New Plymouth (population 75,000), the Len Lye Centre offers a surprising portal into a creativity that stretches far beyond the provincial centre. The building is not only a mirror (literally, given its steel cladding), but also a lens through which one can explore the further reaches of the Surrealist mind at this furthest end of the globe. The Centre could be thought of as a beach-head of avant-gardism at the tip of one of the country's blue-chip dairy farming provinces. It is also a major requisitioning or reallocation of the stainless steel normally associated with the milking shed fittings and multitudinous milk-vats of the district. With its singular and diverse collection of Lye's works and papers, the Centre not only offers a thorough view of New Zealand's foremost Surrealist artist but also an intoxicating alternative to the raging pragmatism and dourness of the province.

A stone's throw from the Tasman Sea, the Centre adjoins the Govett-Brewster Art Gallery – a notable contemporary art space – with which it shares a foyer. Cleverly, given the absence of any immediately apparent windows, the new building imparts a sense of looking outwards. Its reflective, high-tech surfaces offer a trippy re-animation of the nearby buildings, distorting the adjacent clock tower and neighbouring White Hart Hotel (which, in the best Surrealistic tradition, sports a replica white stag on its rooftop). With its concertinaed walls, the building is rhythmical, kinetic; the undulating, iambic rhythm of its outer shell is at once statuesque and poetic. Seeing yourself reflected as you drive or walk past, flickering from frame to frame, is a strangely filmic experience. Or maybe it is like being folded inside the pages of a flip-book. When the sun strikes this great, personable structure, the façade beams and it grins. Lye would have approved.

Next column: Len Lye, *Self-portrait* (1979), photograph/photogram incorporating the 1930 photogram *Self Planting at Night*.

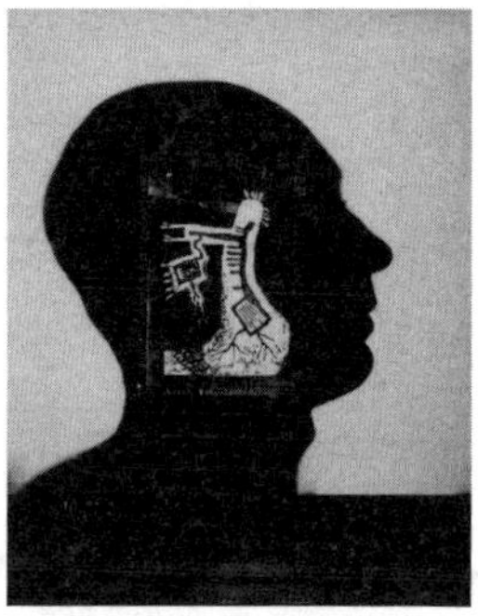

There can't be many Surrealist poets who have an entire museum devoted to them. Lye sits quietly, albeit purposefully, in his three allotted pages of *The Thirteenth Stroke*. (He is absent from my waterlogged Penguin anthology of 1978, by which time he was largely forgotten, except in film-making circles.) Not surprisingly, he had to do a lot more than write poetry to fill the collection store of the new, designated museum.

Shipping out from New Zealand (via the Pacific Islands and Australia) aged twenty, Len Lye spent virtually all his working career in London and New York, where he made a name for himself as a film-maker, kinetic sculptor, painter, photo-artist, book-artist, philosopher, writer and all-purpose mover and shaker. Posthumously, his presence has increasingly been felt back in his homeland – enabled, to a significant degree, by the persistent, lively scholarship and advocacy of Wystan Curnow and Roger Horrocks, two local poet-critics with whom he became friendly during his final years.

Lye might have signed the odd piece of paper but he was never a fully paid-up member of the Surrealist Movement. Writers including Horrocks and Tyler Cann have pointed to his indifference, at times hostility, towards all artistic movements. Cann tells a colourful anecdote of Lye being visited, during the 1960s, by two television researchers working on a documentary about Surrealist artists. He sent them both tumbling back down the staircase of his Greenwich Village apartment.

Yet, long before the recent Carcanet anthology, Lye was being ingested, if never quite swallowed up, by British Surrealism, a movement (according to Cann) 'often characterised as a belated and domesticated version of its French counterpart that mostly relied upon juxtapositions of disparate but conventional metaphors purporting to be imagery dredged up from the dream-language of the unconscious'. An accurate summation, as far as it goes. Lye's art featured in the famous 1936 'International Surrealist Exhibition' in London and a work was reproduced opposite a Magritte in Herbert Read's *Surrealism* (Faber and Faber, 1936). Lye could best be thought of as a fully functioning non-member of the movement – like his friend Dylan Thomas, in this regard.

Lye's interdisciplinary orientation was typical of, rather than exceptional to, the British Surrealists as marshalled by Remy. Lye's colleague at the GPO Film Unit, Humphrey Jennings is included in the recent anthology, as is the art critic and painter Roland Penrose. The British Surrealist poets, let out of the defining jar, spilled forth in every direction – into natural science (Desmond Morris), psychology (Grace W. Pailthorpe), gallery directing, jazz singing (George Melly), mysticism – and just about all of them took up paintbrush or camera. Few appeared to have, or get, or have any intention of getting, regular 'writing' careers. Apart from a few muted flare-ups, the movement was mostly gone by the Second World War, and the practitioners, enriched and with few regrets, moved on. In hindsight, it appears that British Surrealism, like my beleaguered Penguin, at a certain point in its history became intent on eating itself.

NO TROUBLE

Soon after arriving in London in 1926, Lye fell in with a good and dynamic crowd. Stooging around London, Majorca and elsewhere with Robert Graves and Laura Riding, he designed book covers for their Seizin Press and published his first collection of prose poems, *No Trouble*, with them in 1930.

Having been avowedly 'anti-poetry' in his youth, Lye was turned around by Graves and Riding, 'two sensible people immersed in poetry', as he stated in a 1978 interview with Wystan Curnow. 'Then I came across Hopkins, and some other stuff. And sat back and realised there was something really going on [...] I needed the Hopkins magic-stuff [...] Yeats I thought was pretty good. But the greatest thing – set me back – was Norman Cameron's translation of Rimbaud. Boy!' Cameron's versions from the French were so dear to Lye that, as Roger Horrocks writes in a 2003 essay, 'he painted the cover of his copy and carried it with him on his missions as a wartime documentary film-maker so it could provide him with "an anchor to reality" while "overnighting in bleakness".'

Concentrated in the 1930s and '40s, Lye's publishing history was sporadic and low key. However, interest in this aspect of his creative life has grown incrementally since his death. His selected writings, *Figures of Motion*, appeared in 1986, and four of his Gertrude Stein-esque prose poems (first published as part of the sequence 'Song Time Stuff' in 1938) were included in the 1996 Oxford *Anthology of New Zealand Poetry in English*. Two of these resurface in the *Thirteenth Stroke*, one of which is 'Chair in Your Hair':

> Painting painting where is thy mind sting: there there under the chair: not *under* the chair says poppa Cézanne in the legs of the chair says poppa Cézanne: that old chair? Chair in your hair Cézanne Cézanne. A chair in the mind is worth none in the bush. A chair is a chair so leave it there.

Robert Graves, *Good-bye to All That* (Jonathan Cape, 1929), cover design by Len Lye.

Incorporating his own art, Lye's cover designs for Seizin Press and other publishers during the 1930s featured biomorphic drawings and photographs of archaeological/undersea subjects and (as is the case with *Good-bye to All That*) hand-made Surrealistic sculptures. Some of the books ended up looking like chunks of uplifted seabed, coral rock or flotsam. Revisiting such grungy, corroded, overladen subaquatic compositions, I am reminded of my own worm-holed Penguin anthology – my sodden book, my ocean of words – and of Lye's own underwater literary experiments: 'Pearls of the sea / Prayer beads? Seeds of the seaweed tree [...]'

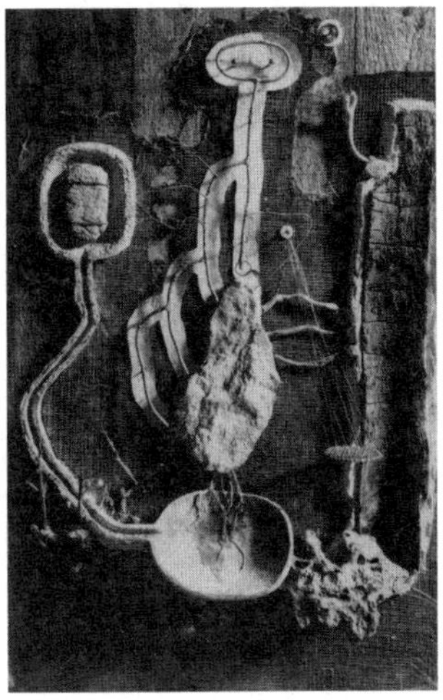

Laura Riding, *Twenty Poems Less* (Paris: Hours Press, 1930), cover photo by Len Lye.

Growing up in New Zealand, Lye had been immersed in and shaped by the natural world. In a memoir entitled *Happy Moments*, he recalled pods of whales passing Cape Campbell, where his stepfather was lighthouse keeper. In that northernmost outcrop of the South Island he received a proto-Surrealist education: peering into rock pools and watching a myriad of outlandish life-forms replicate, mutate, dance and devour one another.

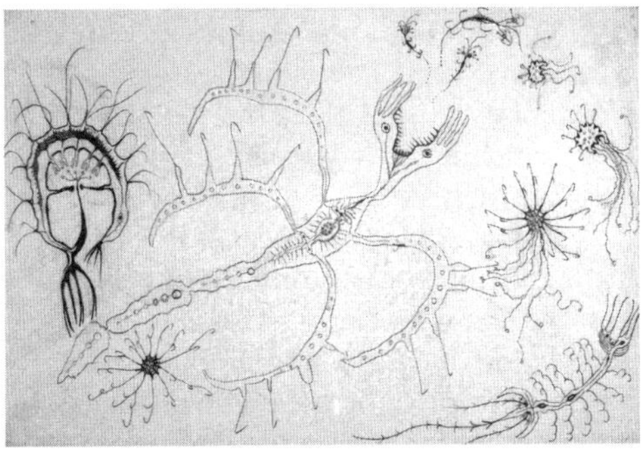

Len Lye, *Untitled (life under the sea)*, circa 1930, Collection of the Museum of New Zealand, Te Papa Tongarewa.

Like the more surrealistically inclined of his early associates – among them Paul Nash and Ben Nicholson (with whom he exhibited as a member of the Seven and Five Society) – Lye was drawn to the littoral and the undersea, although his objectives were more radical than those of his neo-romantic painter-friends, with their moodiness and introspection. Teeming with Freudian/Jungian associations and the violent imagery that characterised his own reflections on the aquatic world, Lye is credited as co-creator of the 'abstract colour effects' which threaten to overwhelm Ian Hugo's 1952 experimental film *Bells of Atlantis*, in which writer-narrator-actor Anaïs Nin glides through a deluge of visceral, suffocating blues and volcanic reds like a mermaid or Ophelia for the oncoming psychedelic age.

Len Lye kept spectacularly interesting company. In the 1940s he made photogram portraits of a range of modernist chums from Le Corbusier to W. H. Auden. Later still, in New York, he took the stage with John Cage, Merce Cunningham and Robert Creeley. Roger Horrocks's indispensable 2001 biography lays a roller-coaster track from Lye's antipodean origins right through these adjoining fun-parks of high-twentieth-century cultural life. In the afterlife, that roller coaster comes to its terminus at the Len Lye Centre – a building which, with its inscrutable frontage, looks like an ideal gang headquarters for the post-Surrealists and avant-gardists of the future.

A FAR PROVINCE OF A FAR PROVINCE

In the Surrealists' often-reproduced map of the world, the islands of New Zealand are markedly outsized – far larger than the diminutive United Kingdom and Australia (although considerably smaller than a re-sized Easter Island). Other countries are strategically deflated and distorted, but New Zealand appears secure and isolated, alone at the foot of the map, as though the rest of the world was just one great thought-bubble overhead.

Mostly to its great advantage, New Zealand is a far province – and Taranaki is a far province of that far province. In New Zealand, we know about provincialism – in both its positive and negative permutations. Out here on the outer edge of most things, it's all we've got – apart, that is, from its attendant states of 'outsider-ness' and 'otherness'. I recognise something similarly provincial in English Surrealism. Despite its proximity to the epicentre of Paris, Britain was always on the outskirts of Surrealism. The 1947 'Declaration of the Surrealist Group in England' (included in *Thirteenth Stroke*) admitted as much when it highlighted 'the apparent paradox that this country has given birth to so many precursors of Surrealism, from Cyril Tourneur to Swift, Blake, Coleridge and Lewis Carroll, and so few intentional Surrealists'. It was wishful thinking on the part of Andre Breton when he pronounced, in the 1930s, that London was about to become the centre of International Surrealism as, British Empire-style, it took over the world.

On the page, British Surrealism feels less committed than its European antecedents. It's more jokey, for a start, and diluted. In the poems and drawings gathered in *Thirteenth Stroke*, Andre Breton's highly sexed muses have mostly been banished and replaced with something closer to a vaudeville show or puppet theatre. (To many present-day readers this will come as a relief rather than a disappointment.)

Having crossed the English Channel, Surrealism had to travel a good deal further still to reach New Zealand. As a movement, it never existed here (neither, for that matter, did Dada, Cubism, Futurism nor Expressionism, in any real sense – although all were absorbed and creatively mined by local practitioners, usually a few decades after their moment had passed in Europe or North America). One theory goes that New Zealand never had an officially sanctioned Surrealism because it lacked a real metropolitan culture – unlike Australia, where a localised version formed before and during the Second World War.

With the journal *Angry Penguins*, edited by Max Harris, as a focus, the Australian version of Surrealism was broad and comparatively under-policed, and incorporated a range of modernist developments in Australian visual art and poetry. A few New Zealanders had walk-on parts in *Angry Penguins*: Auckland poet Kendrick Smithyman and Wellingtonian Louis Johnson (who, a few years later, became a close artistic ally of the young, rowdy James K. Baxter). The painter Eric Lee-Johnson made an appearance in 1949, as did the less surrealistically inclined prose writers Greville Texidor and Frank Sargeson.

In histories of New Zealand poetry, Surrealism, as a topic, doesn't take up a lot of space – but traces of influence or association are widespread. Notably, Bill Manhire's poetry has been co-opted into various loosely-defined discussions of New Zealand Surrealism. After appearing in the *Times Literary Supplement*, his poem 'Wingatui' was reprinted in the 'Pseud's Corner' of *Private Eye*, where it was deemed 'a bit of Surrealist waffle', by Manhire's summation. Yet the poem makes perfect sense as long as you know that a 'birdcage', in this context, is the area where horses parade before a race (it is a 'paddock', I'm told, in British race-speak).

WINGATUI

Sit in the car with the headlights off.
Look out there now
where the yellow moon floats silks above the birdcage.
You might have touched that sky you lost.
You might have split that azure violin in two.

One person's Surrealism is another person's Realism – maybe that's the conclusion to be reached. In New Zealand as elsewhere, the word 'surrealistic' functions, most of the time, as an amorphous adjective rather than a defining characteristic. It is bandied around in relation to Janet Frame's novels and poetry, as it is apropos the theatrical poetry of Alan Brunton (1946–2002), the elusive prose of Russell Haley (1934–2016), and the paintings and poems of Niuean-born John Puhiatua Pule (born 1962), whose youthful sequence *The bonds of time* – first published in 1985 – recently reappeared from Canterbury University Press: 'Fascinating parrots and doves too, fly from the wheat of your palms / straight to heaven. A silent sea / pulls an island up by its roots and / you sleep there with horses from a dream.'

John Pule, *When you return* (2012), lithograph, courtesy of PG Gallery, Christchurch.

Michael Harlow, notable among current New Zealand poets, proposes a gentler Surrealism than most – far closer to Chagall than to Hans Bellmer. With titles like *Today is the Piano's Birthday*, *Nothing but Switzerland and Lemonade*, and *Giotto's Elephant* in his bibliography, Harlow now lives in rural/provincial Central Otago, where he works as a Jungian therapist. Tracing an opposite trajectory to that of Len Lye, American-born Harlow arrived in New Zealand in 1968, aged about twenty. Yet he shares the elder artist's jouissance and a fascination with the subconscious mind, its myth-making and image-rendering potentials – all richly evident in 'The Father Song':

We are the Children. We are waiting [...] Father is everywhere we are not. We are listening to the house grow old. Its spine is cracking. No one speaks. For centuries not a word [...] Grandmother has been knitting for centuries, Click – click, click, – click. Small hills of wool bump the ceiling [...]

A VICTIM OF LIGHTNING

Having driven for some hours at a leisurely pace through rolling farmlands, we slowed on the outskirts of a small nondescript town, not far from Invercargill (birthplace of Bill Manhire), just west of Janet Frame's childhood home at Wyndham, and south-east of Michael Harlow's present location.

From the roadside, the driver pointed out two large topiary creations which towered above a fastidiously cropped front-lawn. (The Surrealists loved topiary, even if they didn't care for the governing classes whose estates it decorated.) Beside a life-size rendition of New Zealand's giant flightless bird, the moa – as tall as the adjacent house – there stood a plump elephant. Both tree-sculptures were perfectly groomed and immaculate in their greenness – apart from one unusual black mark on the elephant's back, which extended down one side.

When I asked the driver what the mark was, he explained that, until a recent electrical storm, this piece of topiary had also featured a monkey, which stood on the elephant's back. This was very high-level topiary. Both elephant and monkey had been crafted from a single tightly-leafed tree. (In placing such a construction within the Dada/Surrealist tradition, I later thought of Max Ernst's *The Elephant Celebes* and Francis Picabia's infamous portrait of Cézanne as a stuffed monkey.)

In the midst of a night-long storm, however, the monkey, which stood even higher than the nearby house, had been hit by a lightning bolt and burst into flames. The fire brigade, stationed a short distance up the road, were in attendance within minutes. Having quelled the blaze, they returned the following morning to survey the damage. The fire-chief told the inhabitants of the adjacent house that if the monkey hadn't taken the bolt, it would certainly have set fire to their home.

A BOLT OF LIGHTNING

With the waves dissembling on the boulders a few metres in front of me, I stand at the base of Len Lye's *Wind Wand* – a 48-metre-high sculpture on the New Plymouth waterfront, a short distance from the

Centre. In the archive, there is a memorable suite of photographs of Robert Graves helping Lye erect one of these 'wands' on a construction site in New York, circa 1960. The pictures say a lot about collegiality and the great Surrealist virtues of inter-disciplinary co-operation and collaboration, with the requisite dash of mayhem.

Len Lye erecting *Wind Wand* in an empty lot in New York City, circa 1960. He was assisted by Robert Graves (in light suit), among others. Photo Maury Logue, courtesy of Len Lye Centre

The New Plymouth *Wind Wand* – the largest to date – was erected in 1999, just in time for the new millennium. Resembling a lightning rod, the sculpture is well placed on an outermost tip of Taranaki, a province renowned for its meteorological hyper-activity, its magnetic mountain – Taranaki, a.k.a. Egmont – massive winds, and weird weather patterns.

Left out in the corrosive elements, eventually most artworks eat themselves or are eaten. To the great good fortune of the New Plymouth project, engineer John Matthews (a key figure in the Len Lye Foundation) and his team have, after some initial tweaking, realised a sculpture which can withstand high seas, salt spray, winds and seismic rumblings, and that it is earthed sufficiently to survive the kind of lightning strike that annihilated a similar Lye-esque, cloud-piercing sculpture on the Wellington foreshore in 2014.

With the Len Lye Centre glinting over my shoulder, my two Surrealist anthologies laid out on the concrete before me, and the *Wind Wand* conducting the wind currents above, some brief conclusions might be drawn – about Surrealism, its various offshoots, far flung manifestations and those things that have been coloured or shaped by it. Nowadays, here as just about anywhere, Surrealism has become part of any aspiring poet's bag of tricks. Writing classes thrive on its exquisite cadavers, list- and found-poems. Yet beyond Surrealism's ongoing application as a teaching aid, maybe it touches on something deeper. Lye and his similarly myth-obsessed friend Robert Graves would feverishly bring their shared ideas apropos the Old Brain to that discussion. Throwing open the gates of his 1978 anthology, Edward Germain asserts that the spirit of Surrealism has indeed become 'the spirit of modern poetry: the search for the marvellous; the desire to break through boundaries between subject and object, between desire and reality'. A useful description of any worthwhile poetry.

As for Len Lye himself, he continues to be an influence on numerous film-makers and visual artists in New Zealand and beyond. His writings have a cult following and a biographically-oriented selection surfaced last year in an accessible anthology titled *Zizz! The Life and Art of Len Lye, in His Own Words*. His work, across various media, continues to manifest an 'inexhaustible power of creating *astonishment*' – a core requirement of any Surrealist work, according to Michel Remy – to which might be added another defining characteristic: effervescence. These are qualities in short supply in the often disaffected.

Len Lye, *Wind Wand* (constructed in 1999)

If, earlier, I found a metaphor for British (or, for that matter, any) Surrealism in my self-devouring book, Lye's wind wand also stands as a useful emblem. As does the Len Lye Centre itself, with its world-distorting frontage. The incendiary topiary of Southland could also be useful. On that note, Bill Manhire, in *The Victims of Lighting* (2010), makes the point that to be hit by lightning is, if nothing else, to be *chosen*. He quotes Randall Jarrell: 'A good poet is someone who manages, in a lifetime of standing out in thunderstorms, to be struck by lightning five or six times; a dozen or two dozen times and he is great.' Therein lies another reason why Taranaki is the perfect home for Len Lye's art – and I'll hold with the literal meaning of Jarrell's statement for a moment. As well as being renowned for lightning strikes, Taranaki is a hub of other kinds of energy – solar, oceanic, meteorological, mineral (there are offshore oil rigs), and seismic. Not to mention cultural (Maori as well as European), artistic, and historical, and the province has produced a remarkable body of poetry. Lye's towering *Wind Wand* stands in the midst of all this like a flagpole – responsive to, and representative of, the forces that surround it.

'Height / is always at the heart of peril,' Manhire notes in 'The Victims of Lightning', then proceeds to offer a Public Health and Safety report on a number of problematic vertical structures:

a shepherd with staff moving among his sheep,
the tall fisherman lifting his rod, those boys
who huddle beneath a tree...
all in their way supply attraction.

Later in the poem, he concludes: 'Nature is full of mystery [...] / we move to close the open door. / Outside, the poet lifts his pen, and waits'. Of course the wind wand/flag pole/lightning rod above me is also a pen. It is writing the sky. It is writing the earth we stand on. And living dangerously but well beneath it, as members of the broad church of Surrealism, we await the approving bolt of lightning.

Some reading

An Anthology of New Zealand Poetry in English, ed. Jenny Bornholdt, Gregory O'Brien & Mark Williams (Oxford University Press, 2006).

English and American Surrealist Poetry, ed. Edward B. Germain (Penguin, 1978).

Figures of Motion, Selected Writings of Len Lye, ed. Wystan Curnow & Roger Horrocks (Auckland University Press, 1986).

Roger Horrocks, *Len Lye: A Biography* (Auckland University Press, 2001; revised edition, 2015).

Len Lye, ed. Tyler Cann & Wystan Curnow, (Govett-Brewster Art Gallery, 2009).

On the Thirteenth Stroke of Midnight: Surrealist Poetry in Britain, ed. Michel Remy (Carcanet, 2013).

Reinventing New Zealand: Essays on the Arts and the Media, ed. Roger Horrocks (Atuanui Press, 2016). This book contains the best exploration of Lye's poetry to date, 'My Word, My World: Len Lye's Poetry', which first appeared in *Landfall* 205, 2003.

Bill Manhire, *The Victims of Lightning* (Victoria University Press, 2010).

Zizz! The life and art of Len Lye, in his own words, ed. Roger Horrocks (Awa Press, 2016)

Wystan Curnow's interview with Len Lye: www.art-newzealand./Issues11to20/Lye09.htm

Visual, verbal and filmic material can be accessed at www.lenlyefoundation.com

---

Two Poems

Tara Bergin

Notes from the Arboretum

I would like to use the arboretum as a symbol,
but of what?

If only I could sustain the energy of my
imagination during religious and bank holidays.

I am afraid of happiness!

How can a bird native to China survive here?

I would like to be able to say that I am unhappy
because of circumstances beyond my control,
but this is not the case.

I look into the eyes of the Saker Falcon and ask:
what did you see in Iraq?

The Saker Falcon gives me nothing. Everyone
wants a bit of him.

I go back to the awful arboretum several times.

This is despite the fact that the entrance fee is so
grossly excessive it prevents me from enjoying
the experience in any way.

Each time I return, I go straight to my scornful
friend, the Falcon.

I look into its eyes and say:

At night we wander freely – half free – at the
sides of our grandparents and among the
grounds of famous American Universities.

I whisper through the wires:

It's hard to know if the dreams are symbols of
what has passed, or what is yet to come.

He sits in his tight leather hood.

Come on, Falcon – all I've got are these notes for
a poem.

Not an actual poem.

Rehearsing Strindberg

Miss Julie enters in travelling clothes.
She enters in these clothes so that we know
that she is going, and will soon be gone.

Miss Julie enters in travelling clothes
and she enters in these clothes so that we know
that she is going, and will soon be gone.

She is nervous throughout the dialogue.

Miss Julie enters in travelling clothes.
She enters in these clothes so that we know
that she is going, and will soon be gone.
She is as white as a corpse, and –
'Forgive me, but your face is dirty.'

She has a birdcage which is covered by a cloth.

Again:

Miss Julie enters in travelling clothes.
She enters in these clothes so that we know
that she is going, and will soon be gone.
She is as white as a corpse, and—
'Forgive me, but your face is dirty.'
She has a birdcage which is covered by a cloth.
Inside the birdcage is Serina,
the little greenfinch – her only friend.
The only one who loves Miss Julie.

Again:

Miss Julie enters in travelling clothes.
She enters in these clothes so that we know
that she is going, and will soon be gone,
and she is as white as a corpse, and her face –
she washes her face in the rising sun.
It's Midsummer.
She has memories of lilacs and birch leaves.

What's under the cloth? What's in the cage?

It's Serina, the little greenfinch – her friend.
The only one who loves Miss Julie.
But: 'I won't leave her for strangers.'
And: 'I'd rather she was dead.'

Again:

Miss Julie enters in travelling clothes.
She enters in these clothes so that we know
that she is going, and will soon be gone.
She is as white as a corpse, and—
'Forgive me, but your face is dirty.'
But she washes her face in the morning sun,
and she is nervous –
she is nervous throughout the dialogue.

And when she takes the little bird out of its cage
she kisses it: 'Oh poor little Serina!'
'Are you going to — leave your mistress?'
And she takes the little bird out of its cage and
she kisses it: 'Oh poor little Serina!'
'Are you going to die now, and leave your mistress?'

And Miss Julie enters – *in an ecstasy* –
inside the birdcage – beneath a cloth –
and 'You spit at me, and won't let me wipe it off –'
and the lackey puts the razor it in her hand.
'It's horrible.'
And the lackey takes the bird to the chopping block.

Again:

Miss Julie enters –
to the chopping block –
'You are too handsome.' –
beneath the cloth –
'I almost fear it.' –
he lifts the axe –
'It's horrible.' –
but 'Kiss my hand and thank me!' –
and 'Kiss my hand and thank me!' –
and it's too late – or it's too early –
and then the lackey puts the razor in her hand –
and –
'Am *I* to obey *you*?' –
and
'Are you going to—?' –
and –

Miss Julie enters in her travelling clothes.
She enters in these clothes because she knows
that she is going,
and will soon be gone.

Again:

Interrogating Shugborough

GREVEL LINDOP

I'VE NEVER FELT quite comfortable with the notion of writing poetry to commission. That daunting phrase from Keats's 1818 letter floats up: 'If Poetry comes not as naturally as the leaves to a tree it had better not come at all.' Still, the prospect of being *paid* to write poems has a strong appeal. So when, in April 2011, I received an email from Andrew Baker at Stafford Libraries, asking if he could commission a poem, the debate was a brief one; really, no debate at all.

'As a Cultural Olympics event I am planning a kind of mini-festival based on Shugborough', Andrew wrote. There was to be music and story-telling; but also,

> Could we inspire some new Arcadian work? What I would really like to see would be some modern Eclogues – ideally with a loose or close connection to the actual landscape. The content could be very varied. Something fantastic – realistic – mythical characters in a landscape – realistic ones – both – environmental themes – poetic themes – who knows. Does this kind of idea appeal?

It did – not least because Andrew's suggestions were so open, so full of tantalising possibilities. I took down the OED to check on *eclogue*, learning that it was 'a short poem of any kind, *esp.* a pastoral dialogue, such as Virgil's Bucolics'. That seemed to give reasonable scope. As for Shugborough itself, I knew nothing about it, though I'd seen its brown road signs on the M6 near Stafford. Googling it, I learned that it was a Georgian mansion and estate, managed by the National Trust and Staffordshire County Council. The photographs were attractive – there were woods, gardens, a river, a nearby canal and railway – and Andrew dangled further enigmatic hints. 'The Shepherd's Monument, with its Poussin relief and cipher inscription, is suggestive,' he wrote, adding that if I were to go and take a walk around the site, the place to start would be Seven Springs, in the Cannock Chase forests adjoining the estate. Seven Springs? Cipher inscription? There seemed to be a poem here ready for the taking.

The idea of playing with the pastoral *genre*, with its ecological, agricultural and political dimensions, was attractive; and I've always enjoyed writing about landscape. Then there was the tradition of country house poetry: Ben Jonson at Penshurst; Marvell 'Upon Appleton House'; Anne Finch on Longleat; Yeats at Coole Park. It could be built on, or subverted, or both. As for structure, I asked Andrew Baker what he thought of

> a fourfold seasonal pattern with some subdivisions? It would give me a clear framework, and the pattern would echo the English pastoral tradition through Pope and Thomson, whilst requiring fewer complications than a 'monthly' pattern as in Clare and Spenser. I would want to use a variety of forms, metres (or lack of them) etc. Does this sound OK to you?

Apparently it did; so we discussed money, settling on a bit less than I'd asked but more than I'd ever been paid for a poem before. Then it was time to visit Shugborough and find out what I'd got myself into.

Shugborough is about an hour from Manchester. I drove down on 19 April, a beautiful day – indeed, an unseasonably warm one, which would later become a blazing, parching, bizarrely *hot* day, quite unlike a normal Midlands spring. If I wanted to mention global warming, I thought, here was the pretext. Early in the morning, and before the heat had grown oppressive, I parked at Seven Springs, in green, ferny recesses among sand and silver birches. Reminding myself nervously that one day a poem would have to come out of this, I began a walk through the forests of Cannock Chase and round, in a long curve, making for the back entrance of the Shugborough estate.

The forest earth was reddish, dotted with smooth, rounded white stones, ranging from pea-sized pebbles to fist-sized rocks: perhaps quartz, though they looked like marble, and were veined with red or pink. Feeling the need for some physical link with this area I was meant to be writing about, I pocketed a pink-stained lump of white rock slightly smaller than a tennis ball. Occasionally among the trees I would spot, half-hidden by bracken, a six-foot concrete square with an iron manhole cover: a capped-off mineshaft. I hadn't heard of mines at Cannock Chase, but the name nagged at my memory. It had associations from far back, and not good ones. Hadn't there been a 'Cannock Chase Murder', or something of the kind?

I crossed a shallow river, glittering in the sunlight, by stepping-stones, and heard a cuckoo calling. The ungainly blueish-grey bird was lodged in a pine on a hillock. Noticing me, it fell silent and soon floated off into the forest. The path joined a road and I found myself walking to a small village called Tixall: just a couple of houses, a very small church, and the empty shell of a roofless mansion up a short drive. The drive crossed by a miniature stone bridge over a gully or gorge full of dead leaves and nettles. Scrambling down into the gorge to explore, I glanced up at the bridge's parapet. Cut into the stone was the inscription 'HÎC VER PERPETUUM' in neatly serifed capitals. 'Here is perpetual spring' – though it didn't seem like it: the bizarre April heat blazed, and the space below the bridge was knee-deep in dead leaves. I found the back gate to the Shugborough gardens, just over a small bridge where two canals met alongside the River Trent.

Shugborough Hall itself was a white Georgian mansion with rounded wings at each side. I found the café (this was a National Trust property after all), bought myself a drink and sat down to read about its history. It seemed the main 'improvements' to house and estate had been made by Thomas Anson, a somewhat mysterious figure (possibly Jacobite, possibly radical) of whom no portrait had survived, though there was said once to have been a bust by Nollekens. Building and landscaping had been paid for with money inherited from the owner's cousin, George

Anson, whose fortune came from the Spanish treasure galleon he had captured during a circumnavigation of the globe in 1742. As so often, civilised elegance had been founded on theft and murder. My poetic antennae began to twitch. Reading further, I learned that it was on this same voyage that the hapless 'Castaway' of Cowper's great poem had fallen from the rigging and been left to drown despite his shipmates' best efforts. This was almost too good to be true. And then there were the monuments: said to be eight of them, scattered at various points around the estate. With a free map from the information desk, I set out to find them.

Near the house stood the 'Cat's Monument': a grinning, round-headed stone cat on a pillar, supposedly a portrait of Kouli-Khan, the ship's cat that had sailed round the world with cousin George. Next I tracked down the 'Tower of the Winds', an elegant stone octagon serving at various periods as dairy and gambling-hell. The 'Lanthorn of Demosthenes' was a strange decorative pillar, apparently hollow, though the wooden door in its base was tantalisingly locked. Some way from the house in various directions stood 'The Ruin', a typical early-Gothic folly (suitable accommodation, perhaps, for a tame hermit); 'The Chinese House', a pleasant, red-lacquered summerhouse; and 'The Triumphal Arch', a fullsized replica of the Roman article, far up in a meadow overlooking the house.

And then, in a shadowy corner of the gardens, behind a colossal mass of green darkness which a small plaque identified as the largest yew tree in Britain and Ireland (again I could hardly believe my poetic luck), I came upon 'The Shepherd's Monument'. An arch of grey stone the size of a gateway framed a sharply cut limestone bas-relief of Poussin's 'Et in Arcadia Ego': a group of shepherds clustered wonderingly around a tomb, one tracing with his finger the cryptic words cut into the surface. So death too was here in Arcadia. And mystery: incised below the image were eight large Roman capitals: O·U·O·S·V·A·V·V – the still-unsolved Shugborough cryptogram. All this seemed plenty to be going on with; perhaps too much. Feeling a little punch-drunk, I drove back through the late afternoon blaze wondering how I was going to get an 'Eclogue' out of it.

At home I plonked the fist-sized ball of stained marble, with its veins of what looked like dried blood, on my desk, frequently picking it up over the following days to shake and swear at as I wrestled with the question of how to start the first poem, 'Spring'. The park wall seemed important: a line drawn between the relative wilderness of Cannock Chase and the manicured parkland of Thomas Anson's ideal estate with its gardens and model farm, now so carefully preened by the National Trust. Much as I liked Shugborough, I had to admit that I found its tidiness a bit irritating. I preferred the forest.

Which reminded me. I Googled 'Cannock Chase Murder'; or rather, I learned, *Murders*, plural: the deaths of three young girls between 1964 and 1967, killed and hidden in the forest by a man who was still in prison as Britain's longest-serving offender. Here was the ultimate contrast to any Shugborough smugness. The girls' names had been Christine, Margaret, and Diana. The threefold image of the girls began to haunt me. Diana... The name coalesced with recollections of the trackways over the heathland. Diana of the Three Ways? A Roman goddess: Diana Tervagans. Origin of our word *Termagant*: a howling, unavenged triple virgin goddess, opening the underworld at the liminal point where three paths meet. (Today, five years later, I look for this etymology and can't find it anywhere: on the internet, in the *OED*. Where did it come from? Did I dream it? Too bad; it's in the poem, for better or worse.) But I had my structure now: the forest outside, savage and unassuaged; and within, the elegant republicanism of Thomas Anson and his neoclassical house. All of it blazing a little too much in that unnaturally hot April. 'Here is perpetual spring'? Perpetual spring would be an ecological catastrophe. I had my first Eclogue.

Summer that year was mostly wet. I decided early on that my speaker for this Eclogue would be that round-headed cat, reposing smugly on his urn at the back of the gardens. Having sailed round the world with Commodore Anson, he would be the journey's ideal narrator. Reading Glyn Williams's account of Anson's voyage, *The Prize of All the Oceans*, I found a story of almost unremitting horror. Having set out to disrupt Spanish trade in the New World with a squadron of six ships and 1854 men, Anson had staggered back, via China, with a single ship and 188 men – plus a captured Spanish galleon full of gold: a lucky haul which was held to transform the whole shambles into a roaring success. Men had died in droves from typhus, dysentery and scurvey; ships had been sunk by storms and collisions. Rounding Cape Horn, Anson's ship, the *Centurion*, had masts smashed and sails ripped off by furious gales: Anson could only keep his ship moving and steerable by making his starving crew, in freezing temperatures, climb what was left of the rigging and use their own bodies to catch the wind.

The turning point came when by chance Anson encountered a Spanish treasure-galleon heading from Peru to Manila. Poorly-armed and unsuspecting, the galleon was no match for Anson's cannon, and soon its decks were awash with blood, 'covered with carcasses, entrails and dismembered limbs'. Reaching home with the resulting booty, Anson was greeted as a hero; carts of precious metal were paraded through the streets of London on their way to the Royal Mint for coining. But George Anson died soon afterwards and his share of the loot, inherited by cousin Thomas Anson, financed the improvements to Shugborough.

As I studied this disquieting history (it was August 2011) the urban riots began, first in London and then across the country. The TV news filled with images of burning buildings and crowds smashing shop windows. In the background, the financial crisis was in full swing. Money, and the violence surrounding money, would clearly be the theme of my summer eclogue, with the suave stone cat watching it all from his privileged seat on the stone urn.

It was in the autumn that sunny weather returned at last: a St Martin's Summer that enabled me to lapse into reflective pastoral mode. I thought of Marvell's 'Damon the Mower' and gently updated him ('The mower with his yellow ear-protectors / guides his roaring four-wheeled Ransome – / smell of oil and cut grass in his wake') and I explored the walled gardens.

Staring into an extensive waterless pond with brick edges ('Dry the pool, dry concrete, brown edged') I had to resist a temptation to rewrite *Four Quartets*; but also became conscious for the first time of just how far Eliot's poem was itself a set of seasonal eclogues. Autumn, with its tinge of melancholy, seemed the right time too to reflect on the mysterious 'Shepherd's Monument' – the stone bas-relief of Poussin's 'Et in Arcadia Ego' with its inscrutable caption. I gave up on the cryptogram: two and a half centuries of ingenuity – most recently on the part of Dan Brown enthusiasts – having failed to solve it, I doubted that I could do better. But it richly rewarded contemplation. The Poussin image was reversed – flipped left to right – making the carving a stone mirror of the original painting. And there was an implied message from Thomas Anson himself: after all, this estate was *his* Arcadia. The monument was the dark spot in the bright composition, the teasing secret door into his private world. It seemed an essential focus of the whole enterprise: art confronting the mystery of death. There remained, nearby, the shadowy green dome of the Great Yew. From the lawn it simply looked like a very large, rather shaggy hedge. Parting the fronds I gazed into a dusty labyrinth of tangled branches folding in and in until the eye lost itself in darkness: a dry fantasy forest that might have been imagined by Tolkien or Ballard. I was determined to get in, and so I did, crawling under the rope a few yards inside the canopy which was evidently meant to keep people like me out. There was no question of reaching the middle: the branches were too close-set, the innumerable broken twigs too spiny and threatening. I found some of the pinkish-vermilion arils (cuplike 'berries' that surround but do not enclose the seed) and, remembering that though yew seeds are deadly poisonous the red flesh is edible, carefully extracted the dark green seeds – one has to peel them out from the rather tenacious skin – and ate a few of the squashy, sickly-sweet things with a delightful sense of transgression, feeling (despite my knowledge) that perhaps I would die. I didn't; but nor did I find a way of fitting my yew-berry snack into the poem. Eventually it became a separate poem, 'Aril'.

Three 'Eclogues' were now in rough draft. I tinkered with them, waiting for winter. It was a long time coming. November and December went by mild and wet, a blurred extension of autumn. January offered neither frost nor snow. I started to wonder what I should do if really cold weather never came at all. I could see two choices: to use the absence of extreme cold to foreground the theme of climate change, deliberately violating the traditional pattern – no 'see[ing] the snow in feathers pass / Winnowing by the window-glass' with Clare; no trees 'with dangling ice all horrid' like Thomson's – or I could make it up, imposing an imaginary winter on Shugborough. I was reluctant to do that, and I was still hesitating when, late on 6 February, the temperature dropped and it started to snow. At last! Now my concern was the opposite: I wanted snow, but not so much that I couldn't get to Shugborough.

I drove down next morning to find the conditions perfect. There was a hard crust of snow everywhere but it was relatively thin: no difficulty walking over the estate (despite CLOSED and KEEP OUT signs, which I ignored). Sounds – a church clock striking the half hour, crows rasping from the wood – rang crystal-clear in the still, freezing air. The Hall itself was hibernating: blinds were down; men in overalls clambered on scaffolding at the back of the house, metal tools clinking. In the gardens shrubs were straitjacketed in canvas padding against the cold. A naked putto and a swan frolicked in a stone basin half full of snow. On the canal at the edge of the estate the narrow boats were locked in ice, clouds of woodsmoke pouring sluggishly from a tin chimney. The carving on the Shepherd's Monument stood out more vividly than ever, its grey stone angles accented by cusps of frost. But in the gorge at Tixall there were clumps of snowdrops flowering among the ice crystals. Perpetual spring? I could already see a way of tying the poem together.

The *Eclogues* were sent to Stafford Libraries in late Spring 2012 and I was invited to read them at Shugborough in July, with a programme of music from local composers. I read the poems between the movements of a string quartet composed by Andrew Baker himself, our audience consisting of whoever from that afternoon's intake of visitors cared to stop and listen to us in the Hall's splendid saloon. (I had brought my lump of pink-stained quartz, and held it as I read.) Once the performance was over and the audience had drifted out to the gardens, Andrew and I strolled, somewhat aimlessly, through the lobby and into the library. As we turned to go, Andrew paused. He pointed to the marble head of a man, smiling down somewhat quizzically from the top of one of the high bookcases. 'I've never noticed that before,' he said, thoughtfully; 'I wonder what it is.' We parted, and I walked out to Cannock Chase. As a ritual completion of the project, I wanted to return my pink-white stone to its place of origin. I walked a mile or so into the forest, found a quiet spot and lobbed it away among the ferns and birch trees. Then I drove home. A few weeks later Andrew Baker emailed me. The bust in the library, it seems, had been overlooked when the house's contents had been catalogued. Expert opinion now confirmed that it was probably the work of Nollekens. We'll never be certain, but it seems likely to be a portrait of Thomas Anson, creator of Shugborough as we know it. We felt as if, in some cryptic way, he had appeared to give the enterprise his approval.

'Shugborough Eclogues' are included in Grevel Lindop's *Luna Park* (Carcanet, 2015).

Two Poems

Caroline Bird

Beatification

My father was a hundred and five years old when he discovered the pleasures of Crystal Meth. At first I thought his gurning mouth and disjointed speech were symptoms of dementia. Imagine my relief when he slipped a baggie of white shards from the netted side-pocket of his Stannah Stair-lift. He called it by it's street-name, Tina. As he lit the glass pipe, he reminisced about a repressed Blackpool girl with the same name he'd courted gingerly after the war. 'Those days were clogged with woollen tights and shame,' he said, his pupils exploding behind his spectacles; 'Can you make me a website?' 'What?' I said, thinking I'd misheard. 'I want to advertise my wares,' he said. 'What wares?' I said. 'Bondage. Water Sports. Sadomasochism. People will pay good money to lick the toilet-seat of a silver fox.' When he smiled his face lit up like an electrocuted skull. 'But you're a hundred and five years old...' I said. He sunk in his sweater like a dying man. '...Which is all the more reason,' I added, 'not to waste another minute. Of course I'll make you a website. I'll even take the photos for you.' 'Will you paint my spare room dark, dark red?' he said. 'I'll buy the paint this afternoon,' I said. 'You're such a loving daughter,' he said, 'I've never felt so alive.'

He called himself The Pounding Pensioner. He was extremely popular. Women and men of all ages came and went at all hours of the day and night. The neighbours complained about the ecstatic howls. The Meals on Wheels bloke refused to enter the house, opting instead to leave the cloche of turkey mush and cauliflower cheese on the porch step. My father didn't mind. He didn't eat any more anyway. Or sleep. He wore his BDSM get-up twenty-four-seven now: leather trousers, dog-collar, studded platform boots. The kitchen lino was lacerated with whiplashes. The last time I visited he was slow-dancing to trance music in the hallway with a young bodybuilder. They were both naked. 'Dad,' I shouted, 'Dad! I've brought you *The Radio Times* and that John le Carré audio book you asked for!' No response. Embracing, they resembled one mannequin sporting a creased shawl of skin. His hearing aid was curled up in the condom bowl like an elf's liver. 'Dad!' It wasn't in my power to interrupt or intervene. I watched for a minute then let myself out. He wasn't coming down again. Not for anyone. He was with the angels now.

Star Vehicle

Can I shoot you entirely in standard definition digital video?
Can I shoot you right up in your gob like this?
Can I shoot you soot-faced and scandalised and laughing on the other
side of the street? Can I shoot you in my trailer with a pet monkey and a gun
resting on a green cloth? Can I shoot you with ketchup on your tights?
Can I shoot you hiccupping in the blood-rain?
Can I shoot you reaching for a metal doorknob?
Can I shoot you running without shoes?
Can I shoot you writhing on a lime and black carpet, screaming
'Look at me!'? Can I shoot you fading in and out?
Can I shoot you suffocating inside a harp case?
Can I shoot you sliding into obscurity?
Can I shoot you shooting up? Can I shoot you shooting yourself?
Can I shoot you shooting out the barrel of a water slide at Fun World?
Can I shoot you on your knees looking up at me with forgiveness?
Can I shoot you on a plinth looking down at me with gratitude?
Can I shoot you on your back like a helpless tortoise?
Can I shoot you gazing directly into my lens reciting wedding vows?
Can I shoot you with a gearstick for a leg?
Can I shoot you pointing at a gravestone with a crimson leather glove?
Can I shoot you with the whores of Warsaw, doing the locomotion?
Can I shoot you after midnight crawling out of a box
with a burnt crack-pipe mouth?
Can I shoot you sweeping the porch of a wooden façade?
Can I shoot you walking down an alleyway with a bag of groceries
looking naïve and unsuspecting?
Can I shoot you every day for sixty-four years?
Can I shoot you witnessing the entire life of a pot plant?
Can I shoot you raising twins, one mad and one sane?
Can I shoot you going through a messy divorce?
Can I shoot you with a rabbit's head on? Can I shoot you re-enacting
a scene from your childhood, unconvincingly? Please
let me shoot you in a nameless city deluged by continuous rain. Please
let me shoot you while you slowly disappear down a crack in Hollywood
boulevard. I so want to shoot you succumbing to a gypsy curse.
You think I haven't shot a lady right up in her vaginal wall before?
You think I haven't shot an addled hooker with a nightmarish clown face
sitting on a molten chair in the shape of a slumped obese man?
Can I shoot you so close your eyeball-jelly glistens? Can I shoot you
making love to a memory? Can I shoot you until I forget my own life?
Can I shoot you on a murdered girl's camera?

'The People on the Lawn' & Other Poems

GERRY McGRATH

The People on the Lawn

The people on the lawn
Were invisible   weren't on
First-name terms with the dead

Waved maniacally at passing cars
Said their goodbyes by postal ballot

Nodded at the thinning poet
Made their own darkness

Were uninterested in the light from Liébana
Fished in their youth

Won countless Petrarchan laurels
Woke themselves from piss-poor dreams

Suffered from chronic distraction
Never knew what they'd missed

Owned a blind telescope
Slipped into mythology

Were doomed to love's sequel
Called the Fire Brigade

Admired the body's embroidery
Were as pale as hosts

Held one end of the silver braid
Thumped their hearts in prayer

Earned long-service medals
Broke wind inside the city walls

Wore rust petals in their hair
Struck coins

Launched a mouse hunt
Tied all their loose ends with logic

Were exposed from mid-thigh to shin
Understood betrayal as
                    a slow circulation in the veins

Becoming man

Con la luz me perfecciono

Come   let me   dip my pen
In the already
                              written
line

*

How can you walk away
    you who are so beautiful

What cruelty
    lets you go

*

A shake of the head –
You're gone

Kick a stone
I'll remember we met

*

Becoming man
May I fall out of love with you
Watch you flying
                from a far
Arc of once desire

your
Kisstaste of almonds
Plumage   a thirst
Slaked in a get-gone dream

*

4 AM
Between a hand   its
              passing shadow
A bronze sky coolly
Enters the room

*

Stays the needling
Spark the page
                manifest
The dew parades
Urgent
                in the waving day

Among Nevadans

26 first lines, headlines, fishing lines

You can only be too clever once

Leave them wanting less

You'll know what time it is by the playground chants

If that doesn't work, ask the dug

A poem should exist

While tap-dancing on the mantelpiece

To be filed under interesting local
flora & fauna

Then [he] Stendhal counted her freckles

Beekeepers of Nevada support
natural human fragrance

Nationalism for beginners – a syllabus

Damaged goods? – You should see the van

The only human awake lives in this house

Extinguish

A pause – let the blackbird swallow its spittle

Oddly enough, a career in marketing

Alder, meet rowan

Sunkissed, eyes closed, water warming to cream

That sound – sawing wood or furiously
testing a zip

Miracle worker shown leniency

Cloud coming in on the tide

Rook at the funeral checking its wings

Gooseberry netting – a poor-looking tent!

Hedda takes a stand
at the school Summer fair

An incredibly soft 'c'

Po-faced conger orders the langoustine

Pigeon sniggers past, tail sweeps the stage
clean

'The Armchairs' & Other Poems

VIDYAN RAVINTHIRAN

The Armchairs

came with the flat and struck on the bolster
produce shimmering dust. No matter.
In them we write. Side by side and facing out
over the sunlit grounds of the college
we're soon to leave for what they call the *real world.*
(A phrase which means to me the civil war
my parents fled; the women in your
books who grasp the thistle of their lives; and not,
as the hard-nosed mocker of our generation prates,
the necessity of moving to London, and working a job one hates...)
But there we are, in the meantime, laptops on laps
and wires happily crossed. Where the silver birch goes
for gold and settles for bronze. Then blue.
Then grey. We work so well together – who knew?

Sea Break

The horizon was pencilled in then smudged
– what of it you saw was through the sand the wind
drew seaward in a white, chiffony curl.
It was time to have, as they say, a conversation about us
while the air turned gritty as a documentary
and the goldfinch bouncing above the rail
brought back last night and all my lust.
And so we spoke but also watched together
this boxset of astonishing weather:
brown iron rusted to the eye-feel of chorizo;
a shattered packet of basmati rice
floating in with the tide we saw turn deep taupe
as the gusty beach was throbbing silver
– the elements taking on each other's colour.

Hail

Down the corridor comes the sound
in lovely spasms – you, typing; I know that strain
like freak summer hail (it's June) clattering the pane.
In the beginning it was winter and I'd stand
once you dropped off and I couldn't
on the landing of another house we didn't own
beneath the skylight at the top of the stairs,
looking up where nothing could be seen
and also heard: rain, sleet; hail; wind, hail, rain.
Then walk, shuddering with relationship
back and forth in the dark before I could learn
the way home to your sleeping body. A game
of being alone and not in a strange place
you're playing now, determined not to lose.

Sanctuary Sequence

LINDA ANDERSON

SANCTUARY

For terrible minutes I searched for the word, like a lost
country; thought of the bird flown into the arms
of the figure my father sketched in a notebook before

he died. *This is what matters*, he said, grief-struck, unsteady,
grounding himself by holding his pencil up to the light
to measure the distance. A room is a place a story

might begin or end, where doors can open routes
to dreaming. I hear a man's voice over the radio
proclaiming desperate measures in Calais, in Budapest,

in Sofia, in Zagreb. I cannot imagine it: a train station;
a wire fence; the overflowing latrine; children playing
on a stony road. The cold distance between there and here.

My pen scratches paper. Words hinged with cries fly off,
come home to roost. I cannot not imagine it.

FIRE

It was because I dreamt it twice it stayed with me:
first the lion roaring at the fire, inside it, yet surviving;

then me in some lonely place, with fire blazing across a hillside
and a forest cutting off the ways I could escape.

My father dreamt of fire before he died. I remember
him waking up, not quite in the world, speaking of how he could

plunge into the flames of his own vision. Fire blinds us;
we can't see what feeds the blaze from underneath:

this is Lacan. He was writing about another dream
and another father, roused by his child's voice and a warning

about a death already past. Always it's hard to know
what's real. One script contains allusions to another;

reverberations, voices, carry between dreams;
sense flickers across what divides us from completion.

LION

To know the language and have time to be in it and to move slowly
ERNEST HEMINGWAY, GREEN HILLS OF AFRICA

Afterwards I searched for the mountains on a map,
wondered if the blueness that we saw through layers

of mist was these, the Kipengere range known also
as the Livingstone mountains, or closer up, Kipa.

At night came rain. Great gusts launching against
the canvas of the tent; in darkness lightning flashes,

our white faces. Hemingway's Africa. Bones strewn across
the sandy flats, river-crossings swollen by rain, the bottlebrush's

sacrificial flowers each day more fervent than the last.
Why should he care if we stared at him? Who was the ghost?

We emerged out of our own murkiness, shouldering the old
carcasses of words, then disappeared into the distance.

He did not move from the track. This slow time was his
to feast on futures. Later he would make it real.

FENCE

I've lived with his fence for a decade now. Six-foot overlap
panels from Wickes in Autumn Gold, sprayed with Cuprinol

to make doubly sure. I've not seen the garden beyond
for years. Not seen the leaves change colour, in spite

of the red berries, their hectic warning. I felt sorry for him at first.
He could barely say 'hello', scurried away when I spoke,

always on his own. He piled rubbish in his garden. Burned it,
a smokescreen, I thought. Then came the first

of the registered letters, phrased carefully, with BSc,
brackets, *Open*, after his name. I saw a window close.

The second letter I failed to collect from the post office.
He added padlocks to the fence, built a fourth shed.

Now he's moving. The fence is coming down. The field is full of lapwings.
What kind of damage needs a fence, a wall, razor wire, to repair it?

Bruno & the 'Bonnefidèlien'

i.m. Yves Bonnefoy, 24 June 1923 – 1 July 2016

CHRIS MILLER

IT BEGINS WITH a French paperback bearing five identical passport-size photos, four of them tinted in different colours, of a man wearing a beret. He stares as though in trepidation towards the spine of the book, somewhat reflecting my own feelings. For this book has a most mysterious title: *Du mouvement et de l'immobilité de Douve,* followed by *Hier Régnant Désert.* The author's name has an incantatory quality that already partakes of legend – I have been told a great deal about him, very little of which seems to me either plausible or perspicuous. He is Yves Bonnefoy, literary hero and friend to that oracular figure of my undergraduate days, Bruno Tolentino. Bruno then loomed over my life like a literary gatekeeper, personally acquainted with authors who were merely names to me (Yourcenar, Bandeira, Meireles) and his recommendations carried weight. So, in the middle of the winter of 1977, I sat down to this little *Poésie Gallimard* edition and the Mercure de France volume of *L'Improbable*, with its classicising font and ineffably French soft cover. Here was an adventure that stood outside any of my previous experience. Bonnefoy's prose was distinctly at odds with the linguistic school that had, till then, been my modern philosophical pabulum. And his poetry involved quite unprecedented arcana. *Douve* was not evidently about anything. It began with the destruction of something like a woman, then moved into a realm of nature infused with eschatological mythology, entered (as I later found out) a locus of Bonnefoy's private mythology, the Orangerie, spoke simultaneously of justice and of mystical love, and issued onto *le vrai lieu* and the poetic voice.

This was deeply suspicious to me; I had come from the New Forest a sort of empirical barbarian, anxious to reduce to my own level anything that seemed to transcend it. Reading *Douve,* I immediately had the sense, familiar ever since, of wanting to have already read what I was reading in order to be able to reread it with greater understanding. I wanted to pry apart each of these images before proceeding to the next yet, before this could occur, I had somehow to accept them for what they were and allow their impact to accumulate. I was reading about a world with which I had little in common, so symbolic as to lack *terra firma,* so formal as to lack oxygen, a thin atmosphere that I could hardly breathe. And yet these images were also working inside me, their rhythms snapping shut in my mind and beginning to inhabit my world.

The house was on a square bounded by the canal and consequently the second-floor living room was full of wintry light. Under the books was the grain of red mahogany. The slightly frosted paper of *Douve* contrasted with the browner, more transparent textures of *L'Improbable.* Over the canal, past the Victorian edifice of Lucy's Ironworks, lay Port Meadow. There I walked or ran, puzzling over this book, the trees now all but bare, banks of mist lying around the river and smudged over the cropped pasture, sometimes opening up to show the featureless, frosty plain through which the icy river meandered. The 'Daphne tree', a willow trunk with arms stretched wide, leant ever further back, dripping with river mists as though metamorphosis implied not only grief but arboreal death. By the boatyards and out on the meadow, I found myself walking through the landscape of *Hier Régnant Désert,* Bonnefoy's second book, with its alluvial sandbanks and distant vessels homing towards the illumination of a port.

The essay that I wrote about Bonnefoy over that Christmas and spring, each sentence considered in the light of its discoveries before acceptance or rejection, seemed to mark the beginning of my true education – the first that I had chosen for myself (the mysteries of Latin and Greek literature had made little impression). Solitary days marked by reading, thinking, walking, seeing – such luxury! That at least I knew at the time. And the quest for the unspeakable in Bonnefoy's oeuvre had elucidated a component of mysticism in my own life. That Christmas also found me reading *The Cloud of Unknowing* and able to relate it to the experience of my own adolescence, of focusing so intently on the Sutherlandish constructions, strange web-like permeable dams thrown up by floods along the Forest stream, that the rest of the world ebbed away, or of seeing in one of the New Forest's meadows by night the multitude of daisies seeming to echo the multitude of stars. I came to understand these experiences in terms of the methodology if not the beliefs of the *via negativa.* And these experiences were summarised in Bonnefoy's words: *Je suis passé de la perception maudite à l'amour.* My 'invention' of Bonnefoy in that first essay was my liberation from what had, in some respects, been a disappointing experience: an Oxford education. Little enough here about Bonnefoy's poetry: as I write, I am aware how unknowable a corpus is in its entirety, even one whose every word is familiar – and his is not: his prose was more familiar and had marked my sensibility at least equally. How often have I re-read *Hier régnant desert?* Three or four times. It had gone home, undoubtedly. But there was a sense, too, of ordeal by obscurity – the fear that, if I re-read, I might find that I had not, after all, understood and was left standing at the foot of the cliff. And indeed, I have had this very experience quite recently, unable to grasp the first sequence in *Pierre Écrite* till a particular symbol dawned on me and I was again released into Bonnefoy's world.

As that world took hold of my imagination, expanded by my reading of *Un Rêve fait à Mantoue,* it entered a series of connections by which a personal culture, I might say, a person is constituted. Bonnefoy came to stand for the visionary aspect of my life, which was often present in the most ordinary moments: symmetries suddenly detached from their context, freeze-frames of natural beauty in the shutter of the eye. Teaching English as a foreign language for eight or more hours a day, I would restore my batteries by running from Jericho onto the towpath, under the rusting turn-table bridge by the station (a perfect background for some black and white urban horror flick), and along the Thames back onto Port Meadow. This run under the riverside willows gathered Shakespearian overtones. Figwort and loosestrife were overborne by vetch and eglantine; dense forests of willow herb and nettle stood tall till convolvulus clambered over them and pulled everything down in an acid scent of rot. Underfoot, the fine particles of alluvium on the river bank joined their texture to the ordered trees, poplars planted along the far-bank meadow like a colonnade, and Bonnefoy's *l'autre rive* became conjoined with a sense of their hieratic order, while the river was *Douve*, the moat separating me from this natural temple. New discoveries were pitched into this accommodating conglomerate. By night, groups of trees were absorbed into long patches of dark and grey, like monochrome Ivon Hitchens, and the reflections in the darkened broadleaves on either side of the iron bridge across the Thames seemed to form Renaissance facades like the empty Ferrarese streets on which de Sica's camera lingers as Jewish laments echo through his *Giardino dei Finzi-Contini*.

Nevertheless, my experience of Bonnefoy's poetry was no longer altogether positive: *Dans le leurre du seuil* (1975), a dark brown paperback borrowed from the Maison française, had come after the triptych of essays and poems constituted by *Douve* ('Le Tombeau de Ravenne'), *Hier régnant desert* ('L'Acte et le lieu de la poésie') and *Pierre écrite* ('La poésie française et le principe d'identité') and seemed to me a disappointment, as it did to Bruno. For Bruno, such disappointments were a regular experience; he was deeply dismayed by Drummond de Andrade's *Boitempo*, Montale's *Satura*, and – to mention another hero I owe to him – Geoffrey Hill's *Tenebrae*. In due course, *Dans le leurre* became a first indication that my literary and artistic gods might know better than me what they were about.

I moved to Paris in the autumn of 1979. In 1981, a close friend, perhaps exasperated by the way Bonnefoy recurred in my conversation, gleefully announced his death; or rather, she wasn't sure; she thought it was him. She was wrong. The organist and conductor Karl Richter was the wholly unrelated deceased (15 February). But under the impulse of this news, the thought occurred to me that Bonnefoy *would* one day die. In uncertain French, I wrote: *Je me fais cet étonnement: je vous écris*. Those who know of Bonnefoy will not be surprised to hear that he replied. My teaching schedule of the time was not demanding but I slept little the night before our meeting as I zealously prepared to expound his work. When I arrived at the little flat in Montmartre, bleary with lack of sleep, I was completely tongue-tied and Bonnefoy tided over my anxiety with a flood of gentle words. I no longer know if I mentioned Bruno's name; I may have wished to meet Bonnefoy in the guise of aspiring poet (I had published some seven poems in student magazines in Oxford). I have retained almost nothing of what he said; I remember above all succumbing to the gentleness with which I was received and laying down my need to show him how well I understood his oeuvre. In something like an hour I was returning to my room in the Quartier Latin, bearing in my hands a copy of *Le Nuage Rouge* signed and dated April 1980. That volume, well outside my means of the time, felt like treasure. The process had been smooth and efficient but mildly disappointing. I had expected him to appear bedecked in the trammels of my imagination.

Nevertheless, I at first laid the volume aside and, with the ingratitude of the young, when I did take it up, found that the first essay, 'Baudelaire contre Rubens', was entirely different from those that I had read; I had no desire to hear about Rubens, whose work I associated with the Marie de' Medici cycle, all courtly flattery and nude personifications so chubby I imagined dust settling in the folds of their flesh. What I wanted was more of the same, and I abandoned the book, this time with the sense that I had absorbed as much as I could from Yves Bonnefoy. I particularly objected to paragraphs beginning *Eh bien*, which showed, I felt, that *le discours*, Bonnefoy's old enemy, had finally brought him low. Paris was full of pastures new in any case. By my second winter in Paris, I had a *chambre de bonne* with kitchen and hallway, painted white by my own hands, sound-proofed against my earlier experience of hearing my neighbour brush his teeth. Here, a trestle desk and white walls seemed to offer the perfect monastic environment for reading. Some three blocks down the rue des Écoles, close to where I had first lived, there was a bookshop with a basement full of secondhand books, in which I had come to place an expectation akin to faith. It had brought me the poetry of Miodrag Pavlović in the translation of Robert Marteau, two poets whom I was later to meet. It offered me a French translation of Laco Novomesky, the mention of whose name later earned me, through a sort of tree of friendship, acquaintances and friends Slovakian and Czech.

Nevertheless, when it proffered a book of Bonnefoy's interviews, I rejected them. Leaving the bookshop, I walked back up the rue des Écoles toward the College de France, and there, in a café on the corner of rue Jean de Beauvais, sitting in the window, was Yves Bonnefoy. I didn't obtrude myself; I simply went back and bought the book of interviews. I found them marvellous. They sent me back to *Le Nuage Rouge*; a new cycle of Bonnefoy had begun and he again took his place among my Parisian discoveries. It is hard to know what so thrilled me in those interviews. I am reduced to looking back through my underlinings to find the occasional marvellous phrase: *Aux fenêtres de l'idéal, le seul ange qui vienne, c'est le reflet de qui s'en approche*, a splendid dismissal of Symbolism couched in terms not unlike those of the Symbolist he had so brutally rejected (*Mais Valéry n'a pas su qu'on avait inventé la mort*); *le ride me ravisse au souffle qui m'exile* from Valéry's 'Narcisse'. It seems extraordinary that I did not then seek out the works by Bonnefoy listed in *Le Nuage Rouge*, especially as the first interview concerned precisely the book that I was next to encounter.

I cannot now date the layers of influence laid down in my mind by Bonnefoy. Those early essays of his in *L'Improbable* and *Un rêve fait à Mantoue* included meditations on painting and on form; friends had introduced me to the work of Poussin; in the period after my graduation, I had increasingly frequented the National Gallery. As soon as I could afford it, I became an *ami du Louvre* and could bypass the seasonal queues. Poussin had become my obsession in this version of the Louvre, which, huge as it was, was not the almost implacably Grand Louvre of today. I returned again and again to *Ruth and Boaz*, allowing the diagonal path to become my route into the painting, leading me from the foreground characters past the stooks of hay onto the road leading to the distant coastline; around it, every overdetermined aspect of the painting would crystallise, leaving me with a perfected vision of the image. Mine was the pagan Poussin rather than the *prisco more* classicism of the *Sacraments*. The *Triumph of Flora* seemed to me perfect. Yet one morning, when I returned to the *grande galerie* and its magnificent line of Poussins, a new one had arrived: a quite wonderful Bacchanale, exhibited without any indication of title. I stared at it, attempting to 'see' it completely, before reluctantly leaving for work. I returned the next day. The painting was no longer there. Was there a catalogue to elucidate this epiphany? In the bookshop, the first thing I noticed was a little orange-yellow paperback by Yves Bonnefoy, entitled *L'Arrière-Pays.* I glanced over the first two paragraphs: above the second was a detail from the very painting I was in search of. (This was the age of paper. Information was not instantly available but had to be sought in libraries and encyclopaedias.) I bought the book; this seemed a further 'message' about the need for Bonnefoy in my life. And now I at least knew the title of the painting that I was seeking, and was encouraged to look for it in the *galerie d'étude*, where items from the reserves would appear unexpectedly and disappear without explanation. I compared these pictures to the ping-pong balls on fountains of water that one sees in fairground shooting stalls. Pictures vanished overnight, swept off their perches by curatorial pellets.

L'Arrière-Pays became a kind of creative heartland for me. I have rarely read it through without interruption; its suggestions and descriptions impel one to dream, meditate, write, create, and travel for oneself, to abandon it for one's own creative life. It tells of Bonnefoy's private mythologies, of the story from his youth in which a Gradiva figure is glimpsed by the narrator and leads him through tunnels into what is perhaps a secret and surviving Roman civilisation; of his own fictions, whose protagonists had heard the *chuchotement* of a mysterious affiliation in art that would lead them to some perfect realisation of the spiritual life. These are the temptations of gnosis, as Bonnefoy puts it; though, in a classic sentence, he retraces his rejection of these temptations, unwilling to dream of *couleurs ou de formes inconnues, ni d'un dépassement de la beauté de ce monde*: '*J'aime la terre, ce que je vois me comble, et il m'arrive même de croire que la ligne pure des cimes, la majesté des arbres, la vivacité du mouvement de l'eau au fond d'un ravin, la grâce d'une façade d'église, puisqu'elles sont si intenses, en des régions, à des heures, ne peuvent qu'avoir été voulues, et pour notre bien.*' I've never stopped reading *L'Arrière-Pays*.

There came a time when France's hold on my life was slipping. I wanted to live in Italy; I was in a relationship that I knew was impermanent; I had a long-standing commitment to spend three months trekking in India, which I did in 1982, so when I returned from Paris to 45 Walton St, I brought my belongings with me, putting off the task of job-seeking in Italy till the following summer, when I would tour the universities in search of a post as *lettore.* My life did not proceed along the lines foreseen and after working in Copenhagen for a season and failing to find that Italian job, I was still in the shared house when *Verse* magazine, then nascent and based in Oxford, announced that it would hold a poetry festival and asked for help inviting and hosting the poets. I can't remember whether I suggested Yves Bonnefoy but I believe I composed and sent the invitation; I know that I hosted him overnight. My programme for the Verse Festival gives the date as 13 June and I think the year must have been 1985.

So on 12 June, I found myself at Oxford coach station, waiting for Yves Bonnefoy to arrive from the Cambridge Poetry Festival. He wanted first to drop in to the Ashmolean Museum and verify the authenticity of a little Pietro Testa painting; I was left standing outside with his suitcase till he emerged relatively few minutes later with a positive verdict that astonished me – could an expertise be so expeditious? (The Testa in the Ashmolean is very distinctive, as I later discovered.) My expectation was that Yves would be swept off to a dinner at All Souls but it turned out that he had no appointments and so we had dinner together in the slightly disgraceful basement – which remained, in 2014, when I visited it with Bruno's biographer, exactly as it was when I lived there, the dried-out plaster ready to pour out of the wall if the wallpaper was pierced. I was still intensely self-conscious in Bonnefoy's presence but improving and had many questions to ask. I made a few notes afterwards, not so many as one might expect; the great poets of the twentieth century were not in the house every day. I remember a savage dismissal of one of his near-contemporaries – *Il s'adonne de temps en temps à un acte de poésie – d'ailleurs on ne croit plus à son histoire. C'est l'acte conjugal.* There was a paean of praise for Jouve, especially *Sueurs de Sang*, *Les Noces* and the *La Vierge de Paris*; Jouve was the best French poet since Mallarmé and Baudelaire. He shared my feeling of perplexity about André du Bouchet (as had Bruno – 'I never really got that stuff'), said how important London and the National Gallery had been for him in his twenties, especially the Italian collection. He had recently reread all of Valéry's poetry and *Charmes* seemed to him especially *passé.* But *puisque vous me relancez sur ce sujet,* he would perhaps write about it again. Famous writer meets younger fan: the things that I was talking about, already some ten years old in my life, were, he explained, some thirty years old in his. And, true to type, when we spoke of the estrangement of the poet from society in the twentieth century (here Celan was mentioned), he said that the reverse was true: 'The twentieth century had expelled itself from the *maison de la présence, la maison de l'être.*' There was a moment when I was talking about *Mercian Hymns* and, trying to specify the period from which those poems so wildly varied, was suddenly at a loss: he gently inserted the word 'Anglo-Saxon'.

The following day, the readings took place in

Mordan Hall at Lady Margaret Hall. Bonnefoy was preceded by John Ashbery and succeeded by Douglas Dunn. It was my job to introduce him; I had a strong aversion to Ashbery's imitation of human discourse and the two collocations (Dunn's early poetry was, I felt, a kind of glum 'social' Larkitudinising) seemed to me little less than blasphemous. I took no notes, perhaps expecting inspiration to strike. But the time came and, Ashbery having been announced as needing no introduction, as far as I remember, I strode toward the edge of the stage (was there a stage?) and declared that, if Ashbery needed no introduction, Bonnefoy certainly needed none, after which it seemed illogical to continue. I think I was called to order by Robert Crawford, who asked if I did not perhaps have some information to add. The next thing that I remember is waiting with Bonnefoy for his coach to London; I think he would have been happy to be left alone but I wanted to be allowed to translate 'le chant de Sauvegarde' from *Hier régnant desert,* to which he reluctantly agreed. I did indeed translate the first poem. Shortly afterwards, I received a little bread-and-butter letter, thanking me for my hospitality, delivered almost in self-pastiche: *Longtemps je me souviendrai de ces pierres, de ces arbres.*

I couldn't keep up with Bonnefoy's productions but began reading more recent works, though convinced the initial trilogy was the essence. I became a more convinced reader of *Dans le leurre du seuil,* to the point where its opening sequence came to seem one of the key passages in Bonnefoy's work. *Rue traversière,* the second volume of *Récits en rêve,* carried particular fascination. I began to dream Bonnefoy dreams, always woven into with that Bonnefoyian nexus in my life, Jericho and Port Meadow. In one of them, associated with a lover and a farm house on the far side of the Thames rented by her friends, I was on that far side, looking across to a picnic of my friends on the open grassland of the other bank. There were overtones of a Poussin wash drawing ('Mercury, Paris and Cupid') also found in the pages of *L'Arrière-Pays.* Either I was looking back into life or looking across to those who had somehow preceded me into death and though shades of melancholy attached to either possibility, the sense of the dream was that nothing was lost; the atmosphere had a Mozartian joy; it was some kind of vindication of love over death; the beating sound of the millwheel on my side of the river seemed also drawn from his work, though it is, of course, from 'The Journey of the Magi'.

Years passed. I had lost touch with Bruno Tolentino during my last two years in Paris and had, I felt, acquired my cultural independence. But now here he was on the doorstep (we are in 1986), strangely reduced in circumstances and looking for accommodation. And we did have a spare room in the shared house – the one in which Bonnefoy had slept. Bruno's occupation of the house was extensive; he rose late, ate roast beef around two in the afternoon by way of breakfast, and worked at a table in the shared living room as though it were his study. The household gradually gathered a collection of hangers-on, some of them dim and unaccountable, others more sinister. Bruno, it emerged, had not met Bonnefoy since his Paris days, when he was writing his French book, *Le Vrai Le Vain.* On 15 May of that year, Bonnefoy gave a lecture in the Taylorian Institute at Oxford, and I watched from a distance as he turned in some surprise to greet this long-lost figure. Life in 45 Walton Street had become rather colourful. Bruno seemed to have mesmerised a Colombian businessman, Edgar, who had little or no English, and he too stayed in the house as if captive. Sometimes wearing his voodoo paper hat like an esoteric chef, Bruno complained of declining cultural standards (Glass's *Akhnaten*). His lifestyle was supported by immaculately dressed visitors bringing wads of notes in brown paper bags. We should surely have foreseen what occurred on 2 September '87 (I had, by then, moved out): Customs and Excise arrived to search the house after Bruno's arrest at Heathrow for cocaine smuggling. He had, characteristically, consulted a seer about the prospects of his final smuggling venture, and had been told to beware of men in uniform; it turned out that the seer was married to one of these and her professional confidentiality did not extend to criminal enterprise. Bruno had, as usual, transcended fiction. He was convicted and sentenced, spending some years in Dartmoor prison, which allegedly formed the basis of his 1995 volume, *A Balada do Cárcere.* Expelled from the UK on his release, he went on to win to the major Brazilian prize, the Jabuti, three times. Not simply by his drug-smuggling, which in retrospect I think he must have thought I knew about, but by threats issued thereafter, Bruno had forfeited my friendship and for a long time I thought no more about him.

The next episode is all but ignominious. *Oxford Poetry* magazine seems to have held a regular translation competition and in 1992 the poem to be translated was Bonnefoy's 'La voix, qui a repris' from *Ce qui fut sans lumière.* I submitted a version; the competition was judged by Michael Edwards, now the first English member of the Académie française, and I won £25 and publication in *OP* VI.3, Summer 1992. Since one of the editors lived in the same street, I invited her to dinner. The spectacle of a man in his mid-thirties still living in a shared student house may have seemed to her sinister and my conversation about drug-smuggling poets and the decline of morals no better. I never heard from her again.

In 1997, Bonnefoy visited Oxford for a celebration of translation, one of the TRIO colloquia organised by Edith McMorran. I was uncertain whether Bonnefoy would even remember me but he declared with some amusement that I hadn't changed at all. Michael Edwards and Anthony Rudolf were also there. I have two strong memories of this event. The first is of Bonnefoy reading out the opening section of *Dans le leurre du seuil* and my reaction to it; though I had, yet again, begun to think that I had exhausted my interest in him, when I heard the poem –

> *Mais non, toujours,*
> *D'un déploiement de l'aile de l'impossible,*
> *Tu t'éveilles, avec un cri,*
> *Du lieu, qui n'est qu'un rêve*

– I reacted intensely, literally sweating with pleasure. This poetry was 'mine'. But the reading also featured Bonnefoy's Yeats translations. I had low expectations; the Bonnefoy component in his translations had always seemed to me excessive, his own slower rhythms overlaying the original. Was it on this occasion that Bonnefoy spoke about 'Sailing to Byzantium', a title that could not, he said, be rendered into French? He offered various possibilities such as *Faire voile vers Byzance* and (more humorously) *Vogue la galère* before concluding that the title should be 'Byzance, l'autre rive', again close to self-pastiche. At all events, I heard the rhythms of Yeats in some ghostly echo behind the rhythms and style of Bonnefoy, an intensely moving effect as though ruins had reconstituted themselves and stood intact but dimly visible through an opaque medium.

And now a jump of many years. With the advent of the internet and my slightly improved Portuguese I had begun to feel a middle-aged curiosity about the drug-smuggling poet who had influenced my younger self, and to follow Bruno's skirmishes with the Brazilian cultural establishment; his lies, provocations and his notorious assault on the Concretistas. This may be the moment to add that Bruno was (a tendency exacerbated by the years) a pathological liar and anything he said had to be tested before it was believed. Therein lay the mystery of the man. One is not cognitively organised to deal with liars. Sometimes a lie came to light only after many years; I long thought one of his friends was, as he had said, the grand-daughter of René Char. I was therefore in a position analogous to that of his Brazilian critics, wondering whether he had really known much of the European intelligentsia of the sixties and seventies.

Consequently, when Bonnefoy came to Oxford again on 17 May 2007 to deliver the Zaharoff lecture, I knew something of Bruno's 'second' Brazilian life. At the reception, Bonnefoy stood at the centre of a loud room of people, some of whom would approach him; he looked a little tired (he was, after all, eighty-four), at once lionised and alone. Besides, he was standing and almost everyone was taller than him. After a while, I approached him and asked if he knew about Bruno's subsequent career. He seemed relieved to have a less formal interchange. We sat down and chatted about Bruno; I said that I was trying to find out more about Bruno and he invited me to continue the conversation by email. Just over a month later came the news of Bruno's death; the obituary that I published in this magazine unexpectedly garnered me a number of Brazilian friends, including the directors of Bruno's estate, which he had bequeathed to a Brazilian educational charity.

I was then contemplating a collection of essays by Bruno's European acquaintance but Yves no longer had sufficient memories of Bruno to contribute. He did have Bruno's letters to him, dating from the years of their Paris friendship, in one of his archives in Normandy and was willing for me to see these, though not to photocopy them; he wanted to know whether they contained anything malicious and was happy to trust my opinion but I never managed to find the time for this visit to Caen, not least because I could keep no permanent record. (The letters would still be of the highest interest in Brazil, where many who found Bruno's lying intolerable refused to credit anything he said about himself and therefore believe his friendship with Bonnefoy to be fictitious.) And when I wrote about Bruno's French book, *Le Vrai Le Vain*, Yves read the article and kindly wrote to corroborate the theory that it was originally written in French, rather than translated from the Portuguese. One of the upshots of this exchange and my meeting with the heirs to Bruno's estate was the suggestion that they would like to publish an interview with Bonnefoy in their journal, *Dicta & Contradicta*.

I set about this with some trepidation; the little volume of interviews that I had purchased (1981, some 170 pages) had been superseded by two or three large volumes from Mercure de France. Yves never gave oral interviews and only ever answered questions in superlative prose. Was there anything left to ask? Looking through the most recent interviews for material about poetry, I based a series of questions on his answers. He replied very politely that they elicited absolutely no reaction; could I produce another set of questions, as various as possible? I could now happily ask any question that I might ever have dreamed of asking him; from this he selected, creating an almost seamless discourse that he carefully linked to my questions. The result was a very beautiful interview, which has since been published in Portuguese, Spanish and English, and which owes everything to his luminous intelligence.

I had the opportunity to tell Yves how much his poetry had meant to me. There was no reply to these tributes. Though proud of his oeuvre, I think he felt that poetry was as much given as made. Our very occasional emails were broken off by news of his wife's stroke and now by news of his death. My admiration had outlived the poplars (about half a mile from Hopkins's Binsey) spaced out along *l'autre rive* of my Thames-bank trajectory; they had long since vanished, cut down and replaced by willows, and this was already so when I wrote to Yves, perhaps a decade ago, to try and tell him how his work had resonated in a reader's mind. Indeed, that resonance is what I wanted to describe here but the account takes in so much of my own life that it has ceased to be the tribute that I hoped; his work holds to my life by so many strands that it cannot be extracted and isolated. I had hoped, too, that this essay would be studded with quotations from his poetry, as the first pages of early drafts were; but rereading his work simply provided a kind of rediscovery, some parts of it again estranged, others thrillingly renewed. And so I again contemplate writing criticism about his poetry and find the circle complete. I am back where I began, the little French paperback replaced by the monumental Mercure de France *Poèmes*, the lightning still staining the white window panes of Douve's blood.

Why?

Joey Connolly

x to mimic the slow pass
of memory, the glassy recollection of a cheap print
of a painting by Bonnard in the university bedroom
of an old friend. *x* to pass the time:
to go past it, into the space of a page.
x as an excuse to sit, handled by the August sun
on a fourth-story Turinese balcony,
swallowed by the late afternoon heat
and Peter Sarstedt playing from inside,
moving your toes in a pool of shade cast
by the laundry drying on the storey above. *x*
to bring tokens of then and now into brief relation,
a lamp-shadowed, concentrating face into the
bright but declining North Italian sunlight.
x to prove something false about the endurance
of feeling the sun on one's face. *x*
like a gesture towards marble. Consider the way
uv-exposure lifts the tan to the surface of your skin,
as if risen from a health that rests in your
subdermal tissues, coddled around your bones. *x* to coax it. *x*
to winch the forms which once were ships of state
from out the greenish water, which won't
even for a moment quiet into the stillness
of a concentrating face, offset by the cheap print
on a Bonnard picture in your long-gone university
bedroom. *x* to retrieve the slow shelter of memory
and the love story below it,
all the bravura genitive syntax of desire
elected up from the tangled backstreets of memory,
flickeringly lamplit and persistent. *x*
because what else is there to do?
There is nothing: make friends with people
who will only subsequently insist upon
going on to die? Rescue from itself
a society which is constitutionally uninterested
in rescue, a princess in a tower with a jigsaw
of terrible beauty and seven billion pieces?
Cook and eat exotic dishes the subtleties of which
you cannot be equipped to taste? Haul up
the terrific wreck we've made of gender,
sunk into every one of our stories?
Haul that up, again? No, *x* in order
to linger on this balcony, hoping the striking
self-possession of the woman
smoking on the opposite balcony late last
night will reappear, her gathered-back ringlets:
her arms crossing and recrossing after raising her
cigarette to her lips, she reminded me of someone.
x because you have a strange internal grammar
which always uses the second person for self-reference
but also for the irregular but sudden and insistent
addressing of various archetypical
love interests. *x* to bring that idiolected grammar,
that ragged coalition of playing pieces from various
and even incompatible games, to bring it to the surface, like the tan
on the skin of the woman on the balcony on the courtyard,
across the courtyard, to whom you never will speak.
x in digression from your financial
and romantic perplexities. *x* like you imagine

an existentialist might, bent over a coffee table
late at night, partially obscured
by an inherited piano, the lid closed and the key
lost long ago.   *x*   as if every moment's perception
was a new year's 'do' and demanded a new
Auld Lang Syne all its own. A perception
of the host of miscellanea suspended above the street
by the opposite block's many balconies – potted azalea,
clayey spades, bales of cable, grey-mildewed notepads, a radio.
   x   in order to oblige a friend with whom
you frequently exchange work to visualise
a parade of new things – the apparently
random scatter of gothic chimneypots rising
asymmetrically from the terracotta of the opposite block's roof
or the naked body of a shared friend, the bold curves
of his calves, the sweep of his navel like an intake of breath
down towards the gentle axolotl of his penis.
   x   to insist it's okay that some things are
radically distinct. My love for you, for
each of you.   *x*   as if in song, distracted by the song;
   x   because what else is there to do? Watch *Amelie* again?
Mastubate in your flat's communal shower? Fantasise
about winning the lottery, that old story, of getting a flat
in the backstreets of Naples, with a balcony, watch the bats
flicker across the piazza flycatchers all, as if
from that confused movement you could take
what passes for an answer?

Apple Quartet

LISA KELLY

I. JAUNE DE METZ

Repeat *If you love me, pop and fly. If you hate me,*
burn and die, and think of your amour as you cast
a pip in the fire. At my ripe age, I look on wildings

with a jaundiced eye. Once skin was golden
like the future. Fortune is a liar. He the scion
of a rich family, I from strong stock. Such notions

of choice; in the hearth, a pip scorched desire. No ladders
to reach an apple hanging like a heart in hock. I grafted,
kept close to the earth, was nothing to birdsong,

good breeding in every branch to which pickers
would flock. My crown not high enough for sheep
to graze beneath, among village gossip, wisdom of

soil and season, gatherings to celebrate harvest
with cider and song. *Old apple tree we wassail thee*
superseded by reason. Longing for lanterns, ribbons

to tie around limbs betrayed by the aphid's
white ruff of treason. What auguries in peel
can the earth descry? *If you hate me, burn and die.*

II. THE APPLE MACHINE

Where worms, roots and fingers
mesh, the future is buried in an apple
machine: Redlove sliced

for ruddy flesh. No dwarfing rootstock
helped the queen control the apple
that blessed the bough. A poisoned mind

finds time to dream. Dwarfs mined mountains
for rubies – now Malling 9 is paradise
preserved. We scatter before we plough,

discard the fruit that isn't curved
to mimic the perfect orb of the sun;
a diamond bite cosmetically preferred

by queens, kings, everyone. A tooth
puller in a souk in Marrakesh wields
pliers to pluck what fireblight

has undone. Like a princess we sleep
in the machine's crèche where worms,
roots and fingers mesh.

III. HERE, APPLE TREE

Here, branches are stark against white
sky, their bronchial diagram a lesson in
breath. A snared plastic bag puffs with

effort to fly free of some small death,
empty of exotic fruit carried
from shelves, the carrier holds its own

trashed shibboleth. Here, custom rots slower
than our apple selves, rosy at the
buffet, all you can eat for the price of burst

buttons, girdles, belts loosening
at the heart's abnormal beat to a defibrillation
rhythm, a wassail haunting the wind

in clamour for retreat from acres
of sterilised soil. Half-recalled, *If you hate
me burn and die,* blown fireblight,

an orange sun's broil. On the outbreath,
If you love me, pop and fly. Here,
branches are white against stark sky.

IV. A IS FOR APPLE

Abbot's Early, Ashmead's Kernel, Autumn Pearmain
Barchard's Seedling, Billy Down Pippin, Bloody Butcher
Cap of Liberty, Carswell's Honeydew, Cummy Norman

Doctor Clifford, Dog's Snout, Duke of Devonshire
Early Bower, Easter Orange, Eccleston Pippin
Fair Maid of Taunton, Falstaff, Forest Styre

George Carpenter, Gillyflower of Gloucester, Gin
Hall Door, Hangydown, Hope Cottage Seedling
Improved Woodbine, Irish Peach, Iron Pin

Jackets and Waistcoats, Jo Jo's Delight, Jordan's Weeping
Keed's Cottage, Kernel Underleaf, Kingston Black
Leathercoat Russet, Lemon Queen, Lucombe's Seedling

Macfree, Marston Scarlett Wonder, Merton Prolific
Nancy Jackson, Netherton Late Blower, Neverblight
Oaken Pippin, Old Cornish Cooker, Onion Redstreak

Painted Summer Pippin, Palmer's Rosey, Pam's Delight
Quarren Dow, Quarry, Queen Caroline
Racky Down, Radford Beauty, Rathe Ripe

Slack-ma-Girdle, Snell's Glass Apple, Sops-in-Wine
The Rattler, Tinsely Quince, Tower of Glamis
Underwood Pippin, Upright French, Upton Pyne

Vagnon Archer, Valentine, Vallis
Wardington Seedling, Warrior, Wealthy
Excel Jonagold, Excelsior, Exeter Cross

Yarlington Mill, Ye Old Peasgood, Yellow Ingestrie
Yeovil Sour, Yorkshire Aromatic, Zari.

2017 mslexia
writer's
diary

Explore emotional experiences as
creative tools in this unique
product. Part diary, part writer's
resource, part notebook. Perfect
for any woman writer – beginner or
bestseller. **£13.99** (plus p&p).

mslexia
www.mslexia.co.uk/diary
0191 204 8860

'Caprice for Violin' & Other Poems

JODIE HOLLANDER

Caprice for Violin

He was only eight
when he first went on stage
with the Philharmonic,
and yet my brother
stepped into the light
and performed like a man.
No one quite believed
how masterfully he played
Paganini's *Caprice*,
the depth of the feeling
the technical perfection,
'He's the next Heifetz'
Mother shouted out
during the standing ovation.

And yet the next morning
when it was practice time,
brother didn't appear.
Mother marched upstairs
and found him on the floor
playing *Star Wars*,
'Snoop Doggy Dog'
was rapping on CD.
What the hell is this,
Mother screamed at Father,
but Father was long gone
for a coffee and a doughnut.
Get your violin,
Mother snapped at brother,
but instead he grabbed Chewbacca
and fiddled with his arms.
Do you want to be a star?
she asked with false sweetness.
Brother paused for a moment,
Then Chewbacca punched Darth
hard in the mask,
then in his black armour
over and over again.

Mother's Tomato Plants

Save me, she'd say, from your father,
from his mismatched socks, from the strings
hanging from his concert trousers. Oh, for
God's sake, stop fighting with your brother,
he's a stubborn monster, just like his father,
the brat won't even clean up his own room.
Be the bigger person, she'd say, handing me
the mop and broom. And while you're at it,
won't you fix your sister? She cries all day,
she no longer sings, one day you'll understand
these things, she'd say: *You are a selfish girl.*
Then she'd move to her baby tomato plants
she tended to each morning right at seven.
And turning on Mozart's *Requiem in D*,
Mother filled the big brass can to the brim,
and watered each little plant in the sunlight.

Mother's Wrists

How lovely they were,
flexing and then extending,
leading the long bow
over the cello strings.
And yet those little wrists
could alter in an instant –
ripping out TV cords,
yanking shades open,
slamming bedroom doors.
Once those little wrists
hurled a dish at me –
dark-coloured blood
all over the kitchen tile.
She never apologised
for that, or for the time
she steered the old Chevy
straight into a ditch.
After she got sick
Mother's little wrists
refused to answer the phone
refused to answer my letters.

At night I can still see
the thin ghost of my mother
sitting at her cello
beside an open window,
the white curtain blowing,
and those little wrists
leading the long bow
slowly, elegantly –
playing that same music
I knew as a girl:
Chopin's *Nocturne*,
or the *Elegy in C*.

Finding Dad

ADAM FEINSTEIN

When did you stop being Dad?

While we were still puppies,
you stooped for us.
Our skinny thighs brushed
the sandpaper bristle on your cheeks
as you bounced us round the garden.

I never doubted you then.

In summer, you were
our captain at the tip of the punt
guiding us down the Cam.
You taught us to skim pebbles,
brought a hedgehog into the house,
explained how Darwin was right.

At home, you wanted to share:
you trailed a wire down the stairs
so we could hear your favourite LPs.

On family holidays, we all sang
Thomas Tallis canons
as you drove us across Europe.
At night, we listened
in a hug of blankets
as you read us Dickens.
We marvelled at your Magwitch roar.

I felt at peace in your giant shadow.
When did the idol totter?

There were weekend mornings
when you slouched at the kitchen stove.
Your beltless dressing-gown gaped open
as you picked at last night's lamb.
Or you lay on the living-room couch,
a book propped on your hairy belly,
scratched your back with a pencil
and listened to Bach.

You drove me out beyond the Gog Magogs
to gaze at your sour-smelling tubes
spinning in their centrifuge.
But I was sixteen,
your language-student son
indifferent to chemistry.

When did you start coming home late,
the stench of that lab on your hands
and anger in your heart?
You pounced on every sentence
with scowled Socratic barbs,
slapping your corrugated forehead
to mock my incoherence.

I recall none of the words today,
only the raw hurt.
You left me china-fragile for years.

I needed your approval.
At times, you grinned at me
over the dark slope of the Erard lid,
pleased with the sinister lilt
in my opening to *Der Erlkönig*.
And there, in our front room,
overlooking Jesus Green,
you opened your mouth to sing
for once, not sting.

Arnold, wasn't that music room
an oasis for you, as it was for me?

Once you took me to *Don Giovanni*
and, wobbling on bar stools at Sadler's Wells,
we surprised each other laughing
at the tender digressions in *Tristram Shandy*.

When my own son lost his speech,
you and I forged another peace.
You lay propped, loose-jowled
and half-asleep in your hospital bed.
We ridiculed a study
linking autism to vaccines.
You didn't live to see
how reason kept me sane.

Here's my poem:
you taught me science could heal.
There was no time to thank you for that lesson –
I found you grey and gaunt
in the hospital where you
died without words
that wet November morning.

‘Who’s She’ & Other Poems

NED DENNY

Who’s She

after Arnaut Daniel

Sweet precision
of the mind-manifesting
voice of the birds, the luminous argot
blown from tree to tree just as we implore
those whom love makes us see more and less clearly,
you inspire me – whose perverted soul sways true,
straight in its windings – to conceive the finest
call, a chirp with no bum note or word astray.

Indecision,
that luxury! No dithering
could touch me when I first breached the snow
of her smooth ramparts, the girl I thirst for
with a wild intensity that is nearly
unendurable, the shining one, she who
has hands whose omniscience exceeds the rest
as surely as love’s gentlest caress bests a

circumcision.
She clocked me, my discerning
between the real juice and the fake – *we* know
how true gold’s hidden by the lead uproar
of our toys – and as our tongues moved sincerely
she drew her dark cloak of constellated blue
so the boys that speak in the snake’s interest
couldn’t leer at what all babble fails to say.

No spring vision
(birds interpret as they sing)
of flowers limning the unguarded flow
of Heaven is fresher; without her, *L’Or*
gives skin no glow nor JPMorgan’s yearly
profits; within her high castle’s living pew
our seeming leaders might be less possessed,
all who exchange her presence for the Devil’s pay.

God’s elision
in life’s book of our killing –
that only sin – our joy with our sorrow
surely bodes well for his setting some store
by holy communion, wherein we’ll merely
look and kiss and laugh along each bared sinew
as I measure the lovely weight of a breast
where the light, the embodied light, swells its ray.

Ah, derision
for my own solemn honking
bites once more – sound in which we think we go
about the gardens of an emperor,
dreamt court in which we whisper cavalierly
as his money man – and I’d be a fool to
mouth her name and put love to the test:
no saint protects those whose chatter keeps the dawn at bay.

Antimimon

O frondens virga

O greening branch! You stand in your nobility
like the inconceivable inmate of a star:

rejoice, exult and deign to free the fools we are
from the bright shade of the feigned tree of mystery.

Like the inconceivable inmates of a star,
shining with the rising dawn’s calm velocity

through the bright shade of the feigned tree of mystery
where counterfeiters play and none know who they are,

we rise with the shining dawn’s calm velocity
to nibble on the paper leavings of a star.

The counterfeited lights, no one guesses what they are
and the drugged soul is the true atrocity,

rising to be eaten by a paper-grimaced star.
The bloomed car flames with the soul’s ferocity

but the captured soul is the one atrocity,
not seeing the bough’s *come join the grace that you are*.

The bloomed car blazes with its sole ferocity
upon the ailing slaves, the city’s brightest star,

no one seeing its *come join the grace that you are*
conveyed in a gesture that is all charity;

above the limping slaves, the city’s lightest star –
O greening branch! – you stand in your nobility,

saying with a gesture that all is charity:
rejoicing, exulting, freeing the fools we are.

Self-Portrait as T'ang Poet at Dusk

This far from the city one bears no unearthly toy
there's nothing now here or in heaven that does not fly
the blue air's brilliant lamentations are somehow joy

I'm a domestic terrorist a walking thoughtcrime
I'm a coin through whose square pupil you can see the sky
from my star-domed terrace I watch the slow dance of time

a day is the merest gauze in which the night is dressed
what need of many books when I have love's live ember
the world is always waving like a departing guest

the waterfall's catastrophe radiates its white
each ghost-drawn tree's the ideogram for Remember
the unspeakableness of all this is why I write

marvelling how the light can darken and still be light

Ode (Semilanceata 312)

in hoc signo vinces

Each one laughs because it is itself all of her, the
real substantial presence of her eternal temper,
ecstatic in an equally serene and raving ease.

Come to me my lost ones and I will make you antic
that long-unwatched song warbles from the bony dust,
not just the whole imagination's manumission

in thistle-starred fields but – feel! – the wrists' virtuosi.
Praise to the lance-snapping folk of the blood, praise the deep
pouring its dark weather on our brains, the Phrygian cap

lifted in snide greeting when the constant moon is full
(each a child of the feral Word, each the freedom pole
seen by leaf-bearded Rip beside the strange-eyed houses

on the dreaming green). Praise to the disordered, those who
find the broadcast wine repugnant as the sluggish loaf,
the ones – *Nature loves courage* – who'll tune to the forest

her strange grace builds, she who unlocks the night with the feath-
er of an owl. Praise her sky-wide incarnation, praise
goddess almighty in the black guise of a dog

or the earthbound earth-transcending tree, praise the holy No
dealt out without regret to the brethren of the dead;
death rends each breath in the empire that's not ended,

except in that unalone apocalyptic peace
subsequent to the sacrament, Sophia's glowing kiss
silencing the virtual serpent's televised hiss.

Reign

after Verlaine

I used to dream of a celestial bling
and Persian or papal sumptuosity,
of Sardanapalus and Elagabalus;
I raised with sheer desire a star-tiled ceiling
sustained on the scent of silent melody:
the spiritual joy of the flesh's endlessness.

Calmer today though hungrier, while
perceiving that true wisdom is to move panther-style,
I loose my madness by reining it in
without one note of surrender in my pace.
So what if the infinite outstrips me at times?
Consign the pleasant to the bargain bin!
God how I despise the presentable face,
the once-daring friend and all credulous rhymes.

'That crack...' & Other Poems

GINA WILSON

That crack
                  in the wall is big.
And it's growing. I t must be.
It wasn't there at all not so long ago.
I can visualise the whole front
of the house dropping off,
a thick brick slice, into the street
where, last night, the pavement
slumped into the basement below.

Three floors up,
                  my study
floats, oddly serene. I can hear
the tick of my joke battery clock.
I look out on the tops of trees
with surviving limbs. Yet
there could be, any day now,
a horrible falling away,
bits left standing,
me sitting on the edge.

That crack
                  houses spiders.
They run when they think
I'm coming. They shoulder
their way into the terrible tear.
When the wall comes down
they'll go with it, and scuttle
unscathed down the nearest
drain. It's a safer world these days
for spiders.

Photograph with a Very Small Moon

It was still day, the end of a summer one
that people had been happy in;
I wanted its tiny white moon, not quite spherical or
certain
to stay.

I wanted to catch it, lacy, fine, almost dissolving
in almond-blossom cloud, so I tilted the camera
upward. Otherwise I might have filmed

little barefoot girls setting up their lantern
with the glass door and tealight,
friends round the warped table, wine;

not the moon but moths, and slugs
oiling the flagstones. I might have caught
a wind getting up, or the edge in low voices that moment
when darkness plummets.

Reunion

i.m. C. B.

The only time I found myself
interested in going back
to the old school, to reminisce
and joke with people I'd never
joked with when I had the chance,
was when I heard you'd risen
from the dead and would be dropping in
to speak with a favoured few.

Then I bought my ticket
and dug out old essays,
B. Disappointing
A. See me later
and started re-reading in French
'Le Grand Meaulnes', even stretches
of Proust, and spoke it out loud
so I'd be ready, if favoured,
not to be B. Disappointing.

And my heart was beating
like a girl's who might have taken
another road because I knew,
if we spoke, I'd tell you *Never*
did anyone have such faith
in me and ask you *Why*
would I turn from that?

And you'd start rattling
a La Fontaine fable that would
explain everything,
darting round the class
like a mouse, or bird, or wolf,
and I'd find my brain still springing
after yours.

REVIEWS

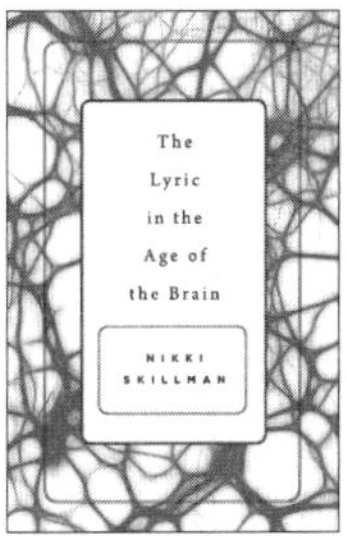

The Muse in Brains

Nikki Skillman
The Lyric in the Age of the Brain
Harvard University Press, 2016
£29.95

Reviewed by NICOLAS TREDELL

'Fool,' said my Muse to me, 'look in thy brain and write!' This might be the updated version of Sir Philip Sidney's imperative for the modern lyric poet, in an age in which neurological research and its circumambient speculations are potent presences, displacing, competing and combining with older poetic, philosophical, religious and metaphysical ideas of human consciousness and identity and offering, with varying degrees of nuance and sophistication, models of 'the embodied mind', generated and constrained by physiology.

Skillman's absorbing book explores the impact of neurological notions on modern lyric poetry, particularly in the work of Robert Lowell, A. R. Ammons, Robert Creeley, James Merrill, John Ashbery and Jorie Graham, each of whom provides 'special insight into the effects of cultural neurologism within a different domain of mental life': 'emotion and personality' in Lowell; 'conscious thought' in Ammons and Creeley; 'memory' in Merrill; 'attention' in Ashbery; and 'perception' in Graham. Skillman's conclusion (which is really the start of another book) addresses what she calls 'anti-lyric' in the work of Tan Lin, Juliana Spahr and David Buuck, Harryette Mullen and Christian Bök.

Considering Robert Lowell, Skillman argues that, in the trajectory of his work, he 'interprets the moving target of his illness' as 'a curse'; 'a metaphysical quandary'; 'a physiological symptom' which lithium could remove ('my own decisive trouble was, as with all manics, a *salt* deficiency'); and 'finally as an emblem of mortal limitation that conducts him, in his last poems, through familiar human zones of hope and despair', for example in 'Seesaw' which acknowledges '[t]he encroachments of our bodies we occupy but cannot cure'.

A. R. Ammons and Robert Creeley were spared the steeps and deeps of Lowell's mind-mountains; but they too confronted, in their lives and writings, the idea that the brain was the basis of human consciousness, and this impacted their poetry. Ammons majored in biology and worked as manager of his father's laboratory glassware factory for ten years; Creeley took LSD and other manufactured and natural narcotics. In the course of his work from *Omnateum, with Doxology* (1955) to his last books, *Glare* (1997) and *Bosh and Flapdoodle* (2005), Ammons moved from a 'transcendental' to a 'somatic' concept of mind, an 'evolution' summed up and anticipated in the poem 'Corson's Inlet' (1965), which uses a walk 'as its central metaphor for thinking' and which figures both mind and poem as 'physical extensions of biological process'. The possibility of pharmacological alterations of such process raised questions about the provenance of emotions and the persistence of identity: in the first part of *Glare*, 'Strip', the elderly speaker, taking a daily shedload of pills, wonders 'if I'm doing / medical emotions or synergetic emotions' and the second part, 'Scat Scan', plays on the brand-name of a widely prescribed antidepressant to ask: 'are your feelings / lofty or zolofty'?

Creeley's poetic experiments in the 1960s and 1970s 'exchanged emotional depth for philosophical ambit' but his late work brings together his drug-induced insight 'that the mind and the body are one' with a maxim of Pound's he liked to quote: 'only emotion endures'. This combination is evident in, for instance, the poem 'Old Story', which likens the plight of a child on a block of ice sinking into a pool of melting snow to the diminishments of senescence: 'so wisdom accumulated / to disintegrate / in conduits of brain / in neural circuits faded'.

James Merrill's poetry shows 'the integration of late twentieth-century biological materialism within an especially expansive creative consciousness eager to situate mind and memory within ancient currents of Western thought'. Modes of loss – for which memory lapse is his primary metonymy – 'populate his poetry' but a form of 'charm' – the capacity both to perceive the charm of the mundane and to charm his readers through what Skillman nicely calls 'his resilient felicity of expression' – temporarily dispels 'the anxiety that the irresistible and ubiquitous encroachments of oblivion – upon the self, upon the body, upon history – can generate within us'.

John Ashbery, for Skillman, offers no such solace but, from his first to his most recent poems, 'extravagantly negates all kinds of mental acts'. She finds everywhere in his poetry 'failures to grasp, retain, and produce information', as in the opening of *Chinese Whispers* (2002): 'I have a friendly disposition but am forgetful, though I tend to forget only important things.' Skillman uses the term 'mindlessness', positively rather than pejoratively, to encapsulate what she defines as 'Ashbery's unawareness, his forgetfulness, his narrowness of vision, his distractibility, his failures of comprehension' and finds his work implies 'the mindlessness', in her sense, 'of his audience', the margins of whose 'ever-shifting attention' is his only dwelling place.

In contrast to Ashbery, whose 'eyes proclaim / That everything is surface [...]. / And nothing can exist except what's there', Jorie Graham wants to see more than surface and feels our failures of attention and perception carry ethical risks for our capacity to care for one another and the planet – risks which poetry, uniquely, can lessen. In 'Lull', for instance, a hungry fox addresses the limits of human cognition and discourse and thus of empathy: 'fox says / what a rough garment / your brain is / you wear it all over you, fox says / language is a hook you / got caught'. Envisaging the possibility of transcending these limits, 'Treadmill' figures life as a revolving road that 'wants us [...] to cast' 'our skulled-in mind [...] / from its encasement / forward' – to imagine 'nowhere', a future that may be 'swollen / with void' but whose apprehension would enhance our perception of the present.

Throughout *The Lyric in the Age of the Brain*, Skillman effectively synthesises close readings of specific poems with plausible mappings of a poet's lifelong itinerary. There are, of course, points to question. Take, for example, her comments on the closing lines of poem 101 of Ammons's 'Scat Scan': 'in / any case, whey leads on to whey and pretty / soon the clabber's all gone: I think I'll take / a stanza break here [...]. / THE BEE MITES ARE A MIGHTY / BIG PROBLEM'. Skillman contends that the poem leads the reader along 'a relatively neat path of metaphors' to 'an untended plot of chiastic nonsense [...] Whatever else the bee mites might signify, their immediate effect and their primary significance lie in their flirtation with meaning nothing at all'. But the echoes of Frost's 'The Road Not Taken' in poem 101, most audible in the homophonic doubling of 'way leads on to way' by 'whey leads on to whey', invite a primary reading of 'BEE MITES' as punning on 'be' and 'might', on existence and possibility, on routes pursued or refused while the clabber lasts. This subverts and revises Frost's portentous lyricism but is not primarily a flirtation with the siren of nonsense. The other capitalised final lines in *Glare* which Skillman quotes, supposedly to exemplify their loose connection to their preceding lines, also seem to connect with the latter quite well, even as they apparently break away. But these local difficulties in Skillman's analysis do not invalidate her general case: after this book, criticism must acknowledge that the Muse of modern poetry is, at least partly, in brains.

Close Reading

Helen Thaventhiran
Radical Empiricists: Five Modernist Close Readers
Oxford University Press, 2015
£55

Reviewed by MARK THOMPSON

Close reading has a history, but can it be written without flattening the details that comprise it? This sensitive account of five pioneers focuses on 'prose and practices' rather than 'ideas and influences'. Actually we get those as well, caught as they filter into the writing. Helen Thaventhiran's critical net is wonderfully fine-meshed. In her first case, T. S. Eliot, she chooses 'the mosaic or macaronic quality' of his early criticism, particularly his ways of quoting (also misquoting) and annotating. Eliot wanted to be 'a modernist critic, not a decadent appreciator', an ambition that entailed resisting the undertow of Paterian aestheticism and the lingering prestige of Arnoldian touchstones. Thaventhiran traces these Victorian pressures with fingertip delicacy. She remarks Eliot's capacity to 'absorb details [...] into his prose, with an effect between quotation and allusion'. In this *between* Eliot makes his way, 'taking on someone else's words and thinking through them'.

As for his 'starkly instructive' and 'excessively dogmatic' side, it does not become oppressive thanks to his relativising tendency, 'measuring particular qualities [...] against each other rather than imputing absolute values'. This feels right; Eliot's discriminations fold over themselves. She might have mentioned something else: he wanted the prestige of authority, and wrote from the start as if he already possessed it. This was a performance, and Thaventhiran is good on the dramatics of Eliot's criticism: staging praise, disapproval, distaste and so forth, often absurdly formal, more ringmaster than RSM.

Moving to I. A. Richards, Thaventhiran sketches what G. E. Moore called 'the golden age of experimental psychology' in Cambridge before 1914. The social sciences had not been compartmentalised; 'students of human culture' (W. H. R. Rivers) could still be interested in everything. Wittgenstein adopted what he called the 'anthropological perspective' at will, for example watching passengers on the bus. This homely *Verfremdung* is nicely analysed as 'making things "seem odd" [...] very much the note of Cambridge critical modernism'.

As for Richards's own ventures into fieldwork, the 'protocols' in *Practical Criticism* (1929) have long been faulted on methodological and interpretive grounds – rightly, no doubt. The book mattered anyway. Thaventhiran says historians 'circumvent' the 'apparent paradox' that the founder of practical criticism was a theorist. Perhaps they felt there was nothing to add. Do inspirational leaders of intellectual movements usually take best advantage of the opportunities they create? It is not as if he was deluded ('I hate the word "critic" myself'). Practicality meant not criticism but agendas for reform, helping citizens to meet postwar challenges. The enlarged franchise of 1918 – almost tripling the electorate – was a spur from *The Meaning of Meaning* onwards ('New millions of participants in the control of general affairs must now attempt to form personal opinions on matters which were once left to a few').

Beyond even this, he was motivated by a vision of social-psychological salvation. Some of his utterances have an endearing dottiness that Thaventhiran might have analysed: 'But when the conflict resolves itself [...] the mind clears, and new energy wells up; after the pause a collectedness supervenes; behind our rejection or acceptance (even of a minor poem) we feel the sanction and authority of a self-completing spirit.' Criticism that is more engaged by systems than examples, and hankers for policy traction but goes unread by policy-makers, easily becomes repetitious and overblown. The paucity of close reading aside, something was lacking in Richards's work, some practice to anchor the 'relentless buoyancy' of his sentences.

The book's heart is its treatment of William Empson. The concern here is his attitude to textual scholarship. Thaventhiran notes the Empsonian ethical and critical principle of generosity: 'to try to make a printed page mean something good is only fair', he ruled in *Milton's God* (1961), which leaves open the questions of who decides on the nature of the good, and how. Starting from Empson's criticism of emendation, she finds an axis that runs the length of his career. Has anybody noticed before that some of the most distinctive analyses in *Seven Types of Ambiguity* (1930) come from the variorum notes in the Arden Shakespeare? Empson told us, but we were too dazzled to hear. Thaventhiran points out the affinity between ambiguity and editorial crux, which the OED defines as 'a difficulty which it torments or troubles one greatly to interpret or explain, a thing that puzzles the ingenuity'.

Bizarrely, Thaventhiran faults the young Empson for not choosing among alternative glosses: he was 'disingenuous, if not plain evasive' for borrowing editorial annotations yet rejecting editorial decisions that plump, as they must, for either/or. She cites Bateson's reproach that young Empson focused on 'what a poem *might* mean rather than on what it *does* mean or *did* mean'. The young Empson embraces both/and, discovering meanings in and around the text; the older Empson often constricts by finding meanings that he already wants there, planting them if need be. Thaventhiran sweetly calls this 'textual idealism'.

Apropos what Kermode called the 'combative rancour' of his later engagements, Thaventhiran singles out the older Empson's 'usual assumption' that his 'presuppositions' are 'obvious and right'. Where the early criticism seeks 'to convince', the latter is content 'to over-rule', and is tiresomely pleased with its bluntness. If his later work still appears generous, she says with lethal precision, 'it is only insofar as Empson strives to be open to the discovery that the author did really mean what he (Empson) holds to be the best meaning, whatever the textual indications to the contrary.'

Examining his 'feats of chatty paraphrase', she quizzes the notion of a poem's 'prose sense' and detects fear under the New Critics' allegation of heresy: 'that prose summary makes poems all too prosaically recognisable rather than insufficiently so'. She is oddly defensive herself about paraphrase, but skilled at analysing its operations and varieties. For myself, I love the paraphrases in *Seven Types* without thinking they replicate the experience of reading the poems. They unfold possible meanings through possible voices, offering – as Thaventhiran says – a way 'to explain poems without falling into the discursive traps of explanation'. I also like her notion that they can be 'forms of thinking, or even singing, alongside poems'. And they can be very funny, in the spirit of what she calls – borrowing from *Some Versions of Pastoral* – 'reverse mock-heroic (applying a low style to lofty occasions)'. In this context Thaventhiran might have considered the mock-juridical nature of Empson's answerable style. His procedural terms ('I now need to consider', 'I submit', and so forth) are earnests of a respect for accountability. Paraphrase can be a witness statement.

The account of R. P. Blackmur won't persuade many to dip a toe in his 'sea of repeated or proximate words'. Thaventhiran wonders whether he was verbose or elliptical (surely both), and claims that he 'presents an unavoidable challenge to readers of close reading', but she means 'to historians'. Blackmur's prose is unlike that of Eliot, Empson, and even Richards: circumlocutory, blustery, oblique, floating high above its occasions. 'Empson's verbal excess testifies to variousness,' the author notes, 'whereas Blackmur's is a single voice repeating rephrasing or circling itself.' His 'criteria for judgement remain', she adds for good measure, 'difficult to determine with any precision'.

This all builds tension: why is she writing about him? She characterises as 'pessimism' his view that criticism never 'tells the whole story; there is always room for more'. (Why? Empson averred the same: 'there is no question of the critics providing a Last Judgment about the works of the past'. Wouldn't the opposite be much grimmer?) She says that Blackmur simply names the qualities he admires in poetry that he likes (by Wallace Stevens, say), being unable to describe or analyse them. I wish she had chosen Randall Jarrell.

The book ends delightfully with Marianne Moore, whose ideal of 'reticent candor and emphasis by understatement' is served by paratactic structures and diminishing cadences, making a principle of modesty, preferring 'descriptive minimalism' to explanation, dispensing 'superlatively faint praise', and a 'lexicon of restrained propriety'. Apropos Moore's aversion to mannerisms, Thaventhiran plays particularity (good) against peculiarity (bad), though Moore contrarily opined that 'we must have the courage of our peculiarities'. The chapter makes Moore more equable and less forceful than the evidence suggests. By recoiling from an anticipated reaction, Moore issues a moral rebuke, unanswerable because pre-emptive. Her quoted strictures upon Stevens are scorching.

Thaventhiran fulfils her brave ambition to give 'a more fine-grained reading of these forms of close reading'. She turns their own tools upon the critics, only overshooting if tempted by exposé, as when claiming that Eliot – in the essay that says 'Immature poets imitate; mature poets steal' – himself 'steals' from the book under review. But he acknowledged the source *in* the review: 'Let us profit by some of the quotations with which he has provided us.'

Equal to anatomising the distinguished anatomists, she writes too much like a committee on human resources, telling us twice what she will do before she does it, and saying 'unhelpful' instead of misleading or wrong. (Teasing this self-protective reflex is easy; no reason not to do it.) 'The point about writing as plainly as you can is that you are testing your ideas against somebody who is not a specialist and just knows about life in general', so Empson wrote in a letter that Thaventhiran surely knows. A book full of excellence, then; not an excellent book.

Yet she is more confident than she feels it proper to admit, which strengthens a feeling that she would rather write something else. 'Not another study of Cambridge English', she promises on page 3. Yet the discussion of Cambridge critics is brilliant intellectual history, and she circles back to Leavis on the last page. The civic vision that inspired Richards, Empson, and Leavis also inspires her. She notes somewhere Eliot's sense of responsibility to the 'dutiful'. With this dutiful book behind her, Thaventhiran should cast off and write a narrative history of close reading between the wars in Britain, and preferably across Europe. Has anyone explained why the finest exponents of these methods emerged in Cambridge and Marburg (Spitzer, Auerbach)? Or for that matter why the best close-reader of paintings, Roberto Longhi, was hitting his stride in the same decade?

From Voice to Type

Nicholas Barker, *Visible Voices*
Carcanet, 2016
£14.99

Reviewed by GRANT SHIPCOTT

Subtitled 'Translating Verse into Script and Print 3000 BC–AD 2000', this book traces the visual development of poetry from its prehistorical roots to its modern, (largely) printed form, and as such has a context in which a typesetter such as myself can find much food for thought. The earliest poetry was not written down but memorised and passed on orally; later innovations such as stanzas, line breaks, indents, capitalisation and punctuation, once unconsidered, became essential tools of the poet's trade. Do they provide effect, or do they intrude? Do alternate-line indents simply frame a sequence of couplets or do they insert a pause... or even suggest unintended meaning in the way that an ellipsis might for some readers?

Such questions inevitably arise as I work on a page of poetry. After more than twenty years typesetting poetry for Carcanet (and others), the variety of visual approaches to a verbal art has constantly amazed and tested me, just as the allusive, metaphorical and personal nature of the language has often left me mystified. If half of the poetry I work on is visually 'neutral', with nothing more complicated than stanzas of regular length, the other half presents features which (I have to assume) add dimensions and perspectives to the language: additional word-spaces, extended tabs and vertical patterns, hanging or stepped indents, printer's decorations, visual tricks with shapes, variations of typesize and style, picture poems... Professionally, I must address this visual aspect while the linguistic angle is less of a concern; in this sense, Barker's book is one I can read with some understanding, even if the text of the poems largely transcends my appreciation.

The first half of Barker's book is concerned with the representation of poetry prior to the invention of printing, and it is interesting to note that most of the visual 'tricks' mentioned above are found in those manuscripts, and to learn that many of these devices are thought to be aids for memorising the poetry. (Some manuscripts, particularly religious texts, were marked up to assist reading aloud.) One wonders whether poetry that was only ever spoken differed from later verse that was recorded in written form. This brings to mind a book I read, perhaps when I was twelve, which took the form (translated from the original Swedish prose) of a Viking saga; certain characters were given to expressing crucial thoughts and feelings in brief, spontaneously composed haiku-like poems, such as this (of two long-parted comrades meeting in a clash of their named swords):

Friend, thy word
Was timely spoken.
Know, Red Jowl
Hath joined Blue Tongue.

My literal, if not literary, mind immediately wanted to know: if he *spoke* it, why is it divided into lines? Why the initial caps to lines 2 and 4? And if he spoke in 'Viking' language, did the original lines also consist of four and five syllables? I only later became aware of copy-editors, publishers, translators and of course typesetters who all contributed their two-pennyworth to the author's own efforts.

Barker's book addresses many of these mysteries for me, prompting more questions for my untrained mind, perhaps the chief of which is, how much is a poet influenced, consciously or not, by the constraints of the printed page? I know, for example, that some poets write poems that will fit on one page; the turn of the page is an intervention that they wish to control. The process of the poet's creation moves from the privacy of the mind to the organised manuscript (still a personal space), thence to a proof, to which only named associates are privy, and finally to a printed – published – page over which the author has no discernible control, other than a legal one. 'The printed page, directed to a less defined body of readers, becomes impersonal, a void that the poet can fill.' A vessel to be filled, then, that can be sipped from or knocked back by anonymous consumers. A far cry from the sacred words recited to a privileged audience in a potentially unique performance. Perhaps this early tradition moved sideways to broadsheets, folksongs, graffiti and other more ephemeral media.

Then there is format. Our greatest playwright's output was collected in 'Folios' which, I understand, were some 13 × 8 inches in size, not much more than what we now think of as quarto in size. For all sorts of reasons, poetry book formats have come down to octavo, although, if anything, poems include longer lines now than in the time of Pope, Milton and the like. I notice that many American publications are more generously sized than British ones; does this affect the average line-length? Certainly the long lines of, for example, Whitman, Ashbery, Koch or Gluck would challenge the British standard Demy octavo page; indeed, I have met that challenge on many occasions, and the most frequent solution is compromise.

Barker's knowledge of the development of typography is deep, and this, coupled with his impressive grasp of the broader historical aspect of poetry, has enabled him to produce an authoritative examination of the interface of the two disciplines. He allows us to compare manuscript and corresponding published edition, pointing to discrepancies of indentation, additions of punctuation (Sir Walter Scott could not be bothered, it seems) and section headings, and adjustments of alignment in order to fit a poem within a given frame or page width. For me, it is an entirely new and fascinating insight to the publishing trade. And, as a final aside, one must empathise with the compositor faced with the heavily corrected handwriting of, say, Coleridge (no doubt with a deadline to meet).

A Handful of Eliot

The Poems of T.S. Eliot – Volume I: Collected and Uncollected Poems
ed. Christopher Ricks & Jim McCue
(London: Faber, 2015) 1311 pages, £40

The Poems of T.S. Eliot – Volume II: Practical Cats and Further Verses
(ibid) 667 pages, £40

Reviewed by MATTHEW CREASY

T. S. Eliot would probably hate the new edition of his complete poems. Under the editorship of Christopher Ricks and Jim McCue, these two volumes have attracted most publicity for their inclusion of erotic verses to Eliot's second wife, Valerie, inscribed within two exercise books labelled 'Valerie Her Book', alongside other handwritten copies of published and unpublished poems. These aren't the only private communications in the new edition, which gathers manuscript drafts of Eliot's poetry and the coterie poems circulated as *Noctes Binanianae* and gleans a variety of verses, couplets, and limericks from correspondence with friends and acquaintances. Such new material may excite fans of his work, but Eliot guarded the shape of his oeuvre fiercely and berated the editors of the *Harvard Advocate* in 1949 for reprinting his undergraduate poetry without authorisation. He also valued his privacy highly, writing to his brother in 1930, 'I should like to leave as little biography as possible'.

This is not, however, a prurient or prying publication and other aspects of these volumes would have appealed to Eliot, who had a keen eye for scholarly editions. The incorporation of intimate materials and verse from private correspondence reflects a general principle of inclusivity. As a compendium of Eliot's poetic output the edition is already a significant achievement, but the comprehensiveness of the textual scholarship underpinning these two volumes is complemented by the similarly impressive scholarship within the extensive notes accompanying each volume. The chosen form of this scholarship is, however, unusual. Most editors limit themselves to brief factual summary, but Ricks and McCue are lavish in the ancillary material which they provide. (Comparison with the ongoing edition of Eliot's prose under the auspices of Ronald Schuchard is revealing here.) At the same time, the notes are scrupulously, even ostentatiously chaste: rather than impose a critical point of view directly, the editors supply facts, citations and quotations without comment. The introductory note to *Poems* (1920) doesn't only contain information about the composition of the collection, it includes two subsections on 'What France Meant to TSE' and his proficiency in French. These consist mostly of quotations from Eliot's letters and critical writings. The acuity of selection here is such that in addition to providing useful information about the poetry, this commentary also functions as a fascinating anthology of Eliot's most salient and compelling pronouncements about his craft.

Despite the general and principled absence of direct critical comment here, it is still possible to feel the pressure of certain kinds of reading. Most usually the reader is firmly and pointedly nudged by the sheer weight of evidence supplied on a particular topic. So, for example, a reading of 'Sweeney Among the Nightingales' in terms of mythical structure by Genesius Jones is recorded alongside Eliot's marginal comment, 'Nonsense', and three or four further remarks by Eliot that the poem was 'simply a series of images'. But the commentary is distinctive too in its tendency to cross-reference matter that may not seem of immediate relevance to the meaning of the line glossed. Consider some of the 'images' from the Sweeney poem:

The silent man in mocha brown
Sprawls at the window-sill and gapes;
The waiter brings in oranges
Bananas figs and hothouse grapes;

As well as drawing connections to Conrad's *Secret Agent*, the notes gloss these lines by referring to parts of Eliot's correspondence from 1911 and 1939 which contain descriptions of waiters bringing items of food. Proximate reference to a window in each of these passages explains their inclusion, since they contain elements similar to those collocated within the quatrain.

There are further peculiarities here: reference to a letter from 1939 to elucidate a poem written around 1918 might seem to violate the bounds of historical probability, but such anachronism is a relatively common feature of these notes. The disposition of the 'silent man', for example, prompts another cross reference to one of the discarded drafts of *The Waste Land* composed not long after 'Sweeney Among the Nightingales' was published, where the figure of 'Fresca' in a kimono 'sprawls / In nervous torpor on the window seat'. The effect is to draw attention to the characteristic rhythms and patterns of association across Eliot's oeuvre and throughout his linguistic life.

The editors don't comment on these juxtapositions, but a model of the creative mind informs this approach which may even exceed in scope what Eliot described as the 'auditory imagination', since it encompasses visualised images too. Outlining this concept in 1932, Eliot invoked the copious excavation of sources for 'Kubla Khan' in John Livingston Lowes's *The Road to Xanadu* (1927). However, concerned to fend off accusations of plagiarism, Lowes (an acquaintance of Eliot) suggested dubiously that Coleridge's poetic borrowings were not 'conscious'. 'Clusters of images' from across the poet's reading, wrote Lowes, 'coalesced' in his mind, rather like people and events in dreams. The form of the notes indicates that Ricks and McCue think something more conscious is at work. Eliot himself wrote:

I should say that the mind of any poet would be magnetised in its own way, to select automatically, in his reading (from picture papers and cheap novels, indeed, as well as serious books, and least likely from works of an abstract nature, though even these are aliment for some poetic minds) the material – an image, a phrase, a word – which may be of use to him later. And this selection probably runs through the whole of his sensitive life. (I:967)

The notion of sprawling may, for example, have been 'magnetised' by the description of Cassandra 'sprawling in the dust' from *Dido, Queen of Carthage*. Noting this echo, the editors confirm the line's resonance for Eliot by observing that he quotes it in his essay on Christopher Marlowe during 1919. Importantly, their annotations follow the catholicism of Eliot's own lead, tracking allusion to cinema and popular song as well as 'high' literary sources.

It's hard not to marvel at the sheer range of reference here, both in the possible sources of influence upon Eliot and in the editors' assiduity in tracking them down. This holistic model of Eliot's mind as a resonant and echoic verbal chamber requires no mean feat of recall and acuity of critical attention itself. The editors are generous in their acknowledgement of the help they received from others (the Marlowe observation is, for example, credited to Anne Stillman). But it's clear that both volumes are the product of a lifetime of careful research and attention to Eliot's writings. Anyone familiar with Ricks's criticism will recognise his closely attentive, interconnecting approach to poetry at work.

This outstanding achievement makes some aspects of the physical format of the edition frustrating. Volume one contains the poems Eliot chose to collect and publish in his lifetime, followed by uncollected material from drafts, manuscripts and the unpublished poems from *Valerie Her Book*. Volume two contains the *Practical Cats*, further uncollected verse and the 'Textual History': an extensive and detailed collation of published texts and manuscripts relating to the poems in both volumes. The uneven distribution of material across these volumes means that, at 1344 pages, volume one is heavy and unwieldy to manage physically. In contrast, the appeal of volume two is not always obvious: many of the poems are of limited interest and the technical information is dense and dry. There are also strange anomalies: whilst volume two interleaves annotations between individual poems, volume one places all annotation at the end of the book so that marrying poem to note is a constant back-and-forth. And if you *do* want to follow up the composition and history of a poem, this is further complicated by awkward juggling between the two volumes. Comparison with some of the recent editions produced by Pléiade (which also include helpful ribbon bookmarks) indicates that they order these matters better in France.

These may seem like peevish objections. Indeed, they should not detract from the extraordinary overall achievement that this edition represents. Like some computer operating systems, I wish it were more user-friendly. But this is a major feat of textual and critical scholarship. It is also a significant gift to scholars and readers alike of Eliot's poetry.

Knowing Too Much

Hans Magnus Enzensberger, *New Selected Poems*, translated by Hans Magnus Enzensberger, David Constantine, Michael Hamburger and Esther Kinsky Bloodaxe, 2015. £15.00

Lars Gustafsson, *Selected Poems*, translated by John Irons (Bloodaxe 2015) £12.00

Reviewed by Ross Cogan

Reading reviews of Hans Magnus Enzensberger's *New Selected Poems*, I was surprised by the occasional slightly sniffy comment. Of course, all the reviewers are polite and respectful. Enzensberger is, after all, a giant of European literature. At the forefront of European poetry since his first collection, 1957's *In Defence of the Wolves*, he is a novelist, dramatist, editor and publisher, and a political and cultural essayist of rare stature. He was a member of Gruppe 47 – the legendary post war grouping of disaffected German intellectuals that included Günter Grass and Heinrich Böll – and established several important magazines, as well as winning the Heinrich Heine Preis, Premio Bollati in Italy, and Spain's Premio Principe de Asturias. The blurb on this generous, four-hundred-page parallel text claims that 'no British poet can match him in his range of interests and his moral passion', and for once this is no exaggeration. Surely he has transcended criticism?

And yet, in *The Guardian*, Sean O'Brien finds room to note, 'It is the fate of some major writers to be tempted into wisdom – the kind that short-circuits the poem by knowing too much at the outset [...] the kind of thing referred to by Auden as "reams of edifying and unreadable verse".' In the *Irish Times*, meanwhile, John McAuliffe believes that 'clear, easily understood and sometimes as easily forgotten, some of the translated poems lack the grip and density, the patterning and thinginess we want from poems'. Something like this may also underlie David Blackbourn's description of him, in the *LRB*, as 'the most important postwar writer you have never read'.

Is it Enzensberger's fate to be admired but not enjoyed? His earliest poems respond to the conditions of postwar Germany with a mordant satire that marked him as an heir to Brecht. For example, the opening poem of this selection, 'Language of the Country' from the 1960 collection of the same name, delights in upsetting the apple carts of Germany's economic miracle to expose the underlying rot:

To be here is glorious,
where the consumptive consumer,
and this is the lesser evil,
loses his hair,
where he hides his successful head
under cardboard and plastic bags,
where absently he calls out from the hole:
here let us build tabernacles

Affected by Marxism, Enzensberger's early work is highly political, and he remains an implacable critic of capitalism. In 'World Market' from 1999's *Lighter than air*, for example, 'Car bombs do the rounds, wives / land from the catalogues, / bank accounts shift by satellite. / Brand new viruses come floating in. / Only now and then by the roadside / there's a beggar lying, motionless.'

It's perhaps hard to love poems that so relentlessly confront suffering, injustice, and misery. Moreover, Enzensberger is formidably intelligent and doesn't take pains to disguise it – an unforgiveable crime. You'll get more from his 'Homage to Gödel', for example, if you understand Gödel's theorem. However, much here is, I believe, just downright enjoyable. Enzensberger has a painterly skill in building up complex images from hints and impressions, and a wry humour that is particularly good on human frailties and ageing, as here in 'Notice of Loss':

To lose your hair, to lose your temper,
if you see what I mean, your precious time,
to fight a losing battle,
losing height and lustre, sorry,
never mind, to lose on points,
let me bloody well finish,
to lose blood, father and mother,
to lose your heart, lost long ago,
in Heidelberg, all over again.

And, though the landscape is often overcast, when the sun breaks through the effect is all the more stunning for the contrast. 'Presumption of Innocence', for example, memorably describes the joy of being so caught in the moment that we are 'happy to the point of unconsciousness' like the 'seven-year-old girl on her trampoline, / how effortlessly, with her hair flying, / she gets the better of gravity'.

I take it for granted that anyone who is serious about modern European poetry should have this book on their shelves (though those who already possess the 1994 *Selected* may wish to know that the first 273 pages are repeated unchanged, and that most of the remainder comes from *Kiosk* (1995) and *Lighter than air* (1999)). Edifying, yes; unreadable, never; he's also witty, ironic and – occasionally – fun. As George Steiner said, 'the reader discovers in him both a satirist and a friend'.

❡ One poet to whom the phrase 'the most important postwar writer you have never read' might be more fairly applied is Lars Gustafsson. Since the death of Tomas Tranströmer, Gustafsson has a strong claim to be the leading poet writing in Swedish. A novelist, essayist, and short story writer, he is better known in the US, where he taught for some years, and where John Updike championed his novel *Death of a Beekeeper* in *The New Yorker*. Nonetheless, it's shocking that this is his first UK publication, and once again Bloodaxe is to be congratulated.

In many ways, Gustafsson's career parallels Enzensberger's. Born seven years apart, both are prolific writers in many genres. Both have studied philosophy and an unashamed intellectualism informs their work. Both are concerned with the search for moral foundations, and both take a sceptical position towards authority and their own use of language. And both have won many prestigious prizes (in Gustafsson's case, these include the Heinrich Steffens Preis, Una Vita per la Litteratura, and a Guggenheim Memorial Foundation Fellowship). Indeed, it was Enzensberger who introduced Gustaffson to Germany in his influential 1960 anthology *Museum der modernen Poesie.*

There, however, the similarities end. Gustafsson's verse is human, compassionate, playful, deeply concerned with the natural world, minutely observant and, quite often, just laugh-out-loud funny. Take, for example, 'Of Course Superman is Clark Kent', an elegy for the great American logician W. V. O. Quine. There is no less promising subject for poetry. Read Quine's *Word and Object* if you don't believe me. And yet somehow Gustafsson creates something that is both informed by Quine's thought on language and representation (it's the only poem I've ever read that contains logical symbols), while also a funny, beautiful, and moving elegy:

'And quite honestly,' the old logician added,
while he discretely brushed the chalk dust
from shy and slender hands that
suggested they had never caressed a woman,
at the end of a long, sweaty demonstration,

quite honestly
I have never really understood
just why *existence* is to be considered so important.
Unicorns, imaginary numbers still do all right,
and Mr Pickwick and all his friends.
Not to mention God.
Of course Superman is Clark Kent.

There are wonderful poems here about music, painting, and our relationship with nature that will appeal to an English audience. The highlights are too numerous to mention, but his meditation on the value of tradition in 'Ballad on the paths in Västmanland' is particularly memorable:

Beneath the visible writing of small roads,
gravelled roads, farm tracks, often with a comb
of grass in the middle between deep wheel ruts,
hidden beneath clear-felling's tangle of brushwood,
still legible in the dried-up moss,
there is another script: the old paths.

These old paths become a metaphor for human communities and their implicit knowledge:

We make it together,
you too make it on a windy day when
it is early or late on the earth:
We write the paths, and the paths remain,
and the paths are wiser than we are,
and know all we wanted to know.

I'm tempted to contrast these two great poets by way of 'Minor Gods', a poem by Gustafsson. Major Gods, 'a Baal, an El, / defeat the Powers of Chaos in a heroic battle // (they think) / and then carefully erect their fortress / on the highest mountain'. The minor Gods, meanwhile, 'the small fry, / lares, gnomes and the little grey wise ones, // dig away in the autumn roots of the old ash / and send strange fungi // up into the light of day. They are lazy, languid gods. // But they want to have a say as well.' Enzensberger is a statue viewed from a distance, raining down his thunderbolts on late capitalism. Gustafsson is, in Per Wåstberg's wonderful phrase, an 'aged faun', peering from the undergrowth and humming his 'song to what has been lost'. It just goes to show that giants come in all shapes and sizes.

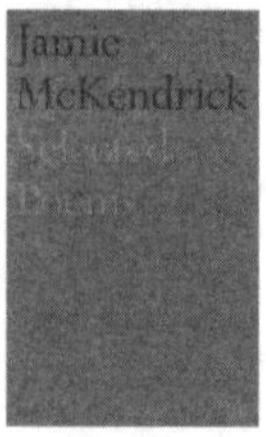

Balancing Acts

Jamie McKendrick, *Selected Poems*
Faber, 2016

Michael Symmons Roberts
Selected Poems
Cape, 2016

Derek Mahon, *New Selected Poems*
Faber / Gallery Press, 2016

Reviewed by DAVID SPITTLE

'Omissions are not accidents', declared Marianne Moore in her *Complete Poems* as a wry disclaimer to her revisionist approach. What, then, of that more explicitly discriminating model – a poet's *Selected?* Should the *Selected* gather the unwieldy corpus of a life's work into a mapped trajectory, a neat phase-by-phase articulation of 'growth', 'progress', and other critical red herrings of linearity? Or, in resistance to the familiar narrative, is the *Selected a* chance to re-configure and, borrowing Moore's scalpel, fashion anew the poet's body of writing? For many readers it is the introduction, the teasing gateway buffet from which to catapult a further and more intensive grazing. They are books that then shift uniquely in our estimation as, while tied to the nostalgia of discovery, over time they can come to feel heartlessly slim and deficient. If the book is successful, the reader will seek out further work and hence later return to find the *Selected* as a diminished token of what it revealed. The following *Selected* volumes attest to the precarious difficulties and possible reward entailed by such editorial balancing acts.

Jamie McKendrick's *Selected Poems* draws from six collections, from his 1991 debut *The Sirocco Room* up to his latest collection, 2012's *Out There*. He is the editor of *The Faber Book of 20th-Century Italian Poems* (2004) and has translated numerous other poets (Giorgio Bassani, Valerio Magrelli, David Huerta, Pier Paolo Pasolini), receiving an Oxford-Weidenfield prize in 2010 for his translation of Magrelli's *The Embrace.* There is a control that governs his poetry with its own gratifying and coiled spring: be it the macabre wit of 'Ire', in which a hoverfly's imitation of a wasp is fatally seized upon *by* a wasp ('The counterfeiter pulsed its flimsy wings / so the wasp tore them out and let them fall'); the lucid abstraction of 'Sky Nails' ('that will nail anything / to nothing / and make it stay'); or the precise and wrenching – though delicately wrought – evocation of a dying fish in 'Fish Eye' ('a fog like a tide of opal stole / over the oily surface of the eye / extinguishing an eerie Borealis').

Yet it is also the precision that so deftly lasers McKendrick's poems with their character that sometimes leaves them aching for a more ragged life. His control and formal restraint, rather than always being a source of finely tuned craft, can become a clipped or politely curtailed style that could provide more. At times the poems seem too content to be snapshots, held and safely captured, when in fact the prospect of them wandering off and out seems much more exciting. One such poem is 'Skin Deep', a brilliantly observed encounter between divers and an octopus that 'thinks in colour':

Beware and welcome have twenty inflections
like Delacroix saying Mon cher monsieur
– for tomorrow's lunch they'll all boil down

to an inky sauce, some Redon lithograph
of spiders dancing in the afterlife.

The eight-legged ghost waltz scratched in Redon's ink is undeniably a wonderful twist of evocation. The writing is not at fault, but its safe refusal to abstain from *more* writing and to end on that image, as a sonnet, is frustrating. It is arguably a strong move to leave the poem's brief description with a sting in the tail – *leave 'em wanting more* – but for a poet who can clearly write with such visual invention and intelligence, the image-as-punchline does a disservice to what, across the *Selected*, you begin to suspect McKendrick is capable of. Also, why a sonnet? Could it not inch its tentacular vision from out of that particular box? McKendrick's portrait feels artfully conjured but stunted, cut off in its prime. The same feeling haunts his eccentric list-poem 'The Fly Inventory':

The fly in the film *The Fly*.
The fly in the remake *The Fly*.
The fly on the frieze in the *mercato di lana* at Pompeii.
The fly that bit the flying horse that caused the fall [...].

The poem is sparked by a simple yet humorous idea, and adopts a rare free-verse flow. But just as it gallops onto a second page, seemingly ready to wheel into flight, perhaps even diverge from listing, it ends. It is kept, sealed and controlled as a comedic list-poem when in fact one feels McKendrick's writing could have steered it into a weird epic.

This frustration that peppers the book is, perhaps, forewarned in the opening poem, '&', which could be read as a prefatory diagnosis. The opening stanza invokes 'A born rebel, at ease in your outrage / you refuse the armchair's invitation', which is then countered by the assertion 'I'm by contrast on a hardbacked chair / sitting trim and tightarsed as Britannia'. The two characters or perspectives constitute an 'argument we're having', now 'unravelling' to leave the question of 'how they ever did get joined together. / It seems we've unwound an ampersand and / pulled it like a cracker'. The rebellious refusal of the chair and the disciplined sitter ('with a shield of books') are then joined 'On the third chair' by:

the black-and-white cat and the white-and-black,
love-locked in a tricky double helix,
keep licking each others necks.

Despite the pleasing wit of the Gordian image and its illustration of the ampersand, there is a sense here and elsewhere in the poems that two conflicting styles are vying for prominence, one favouring unruly defiance and the other prim discipline. While there are glimpses of a poetic reconciliation, this book – a terrific showcase of McKendrick's skill – leaves one hungering for that feline, 'love-locked' enigma, the spectre of what McKendrick's poetry *could* achieve.

¶ Michael Symmons Roberts has published six collections of poems. He a regular librettist in collaboration with composer James MacMillan, writes extensively for radio, and has received numerous accolades (shortlisted three times for the T. S. Eliot Prize and winner of the Whitbread Poetry Prize and the Costa Poetry Award). The back cover of his (it has to be said, handsomely produced) *Selected Poems* is emblazoned with praise from Carol Ann Duffy, Jeanette Winterson, and Sean O'Brien. Praised by Jeanette Winterson as a 'religious poet for a secular age', Roberts consistently returns to questions of faith and the hauntings between corporeal and spiritual. Ever since the formative and early experience of losing faith in his own atheism (which he ascribes to studying Philosophy and Theology at Oxford), the language of science has often lightly grated itself over sonorous ponderings ('Deus Ex Machina I', 'To John Donne', 'The Structure of Genes') as if to negotiate an awkward phone call between the transcendent and the material.

Where others find this particular engagement with religion to be arresting or emotive, Roberts's tone can become, from poem to poem, indistinguishably muted in shades of its own seriousness. Over the book's 150 pages it becomes increasingly hard to connect with separate emotions or ideas amidst the presiding weight of atmosphere. 'Atmosphere' is an unhelpful ambiguity, but I use it to convey the sealed world one seems to enter in these poems, a world too stiflingly enamoured with its own solemn project to communicate its actual details.

However, much of the portentous heaviness that blurs these poems comes cumulatively, not from any one poem but from the awkward demands of the *Selected* as a form. Many of Roberts's books unfold with deliberation, at times ceremonial in pace and measure, to bring their interspersed sequences and themes in step with one another. In *Soft Keys* (1993) there is a cluster of poems on Simone Weil and the Hookses, both reduced here to one representative poem each; in *Corpus* (2004), the 'Food for Risen Bodies' sequence imagines ritualistic meals that punctuate the collection, a formal conceit beyond the *Selected*; in *The Half Healed* (2008) a sequence

'Last Words' is poignantly scattered throughout – here its parts are grouped together; and the echoes and refrains in *Drysalter* (2013), itself an ambitious book-length sequence of 150 fifteen-line poems (nearly the size of this *Selected* on its own) are similarly curtailed. The need to range across these delicately paced and dispersed forms necessarily involves a process of disruption and compression, one that compromises the patterned structuring of Roberts's work. There are comparisons to be made in his poetry to that of Michael Donaghy, Robin Robertson, David Harsent, and more recently Toby Martinez de las Rivas. This is poetry best served in the organised space of its original context, or in the more completist arc of a *Collected Poems*.

¶ While the *Selected Poems* of Jamie McKendrick leaves one willing the poet break out of glimpsed previews into something more ambitious and developed, and while the *Selected Poems* of Michael Symmons Roberts gives the false impression of a sum that is less than its parts, Derek Mahon's slim *New Selected Poems* arrives as a perfectly judged selection. Born in Belfast in 1941, Mahon authored his first collection, *Night Crossing*, in 1968; his most recent collection, *An Autumn Wind*, was published in 2010. In the intervening years Mahon has accumulated a huge body of important work. Despite the expanse of Mahon's achievement, at just over one hundred pages his *Selected Poems* is a joy to glide through from cover to cover.

It opens with 'Gengormley' and the quotidian of mortality ('who has tamed the terrier, trimmed the hedge / and grasped the principle of the watering can') that concludes 'the quick noose of their finite being' to be a darkly humorous space where 'By / necessity, if not choice, I live here too.' This is followed by the elegiac tribute to Louis Macneice, 'Carrowdore', a poem at once sweeping and incisive in its intimacy: 'This, you implied, is how we ought to live – // the ironical, loving crush of roses against snow / each fragile, solving ambiguity'. A melancholy breather arrives with 'Day Trip to Donegal' ('contriving vain / overtures to the vindictive wind and rain'), and is upturned again by another intricately handled contemplation of the everyday and the end of days in the 'An Unborn Child', in which Mahon's light but concerted control of the poem's pace is exemplary of the care and skill displayed throughout this volume. 'An Unborn Child' gives way to a fondly bleak triumvirate of desolation, excavation and deracination in 'An Image from Beckett' ('a northern landscape / and a huddle / of houses along the shore'), 'Lives' ('when the lost ship / sailed away. I thought / of Ithaca, but soon decayed'), and 'Afterlives', which reflects:

Perhaps if I'd stayed behind
and lived it bomb by bomb
I might have grown up at last
and learnt what is meant by home.

Though Mahon's poetry is suffused with the sadness of temporal and spatial displacement, its nostalgia for Northern Ireland as a lost home or excluded self is never miserable. Through a combination of dark wit, stoic humour and the authority imparted by a seamless formal lyricism, Mahon's sorrow goes beyond introspection. His skilled portraits tenderly kindle their own tacit doubles, in an unfurling warmth of something remembered, imagined or possible: 'Dear ghost, remember me without ill will / as I remember your lost mystery still.' This *New Selected Poems* is a stunning and essential testament to Mahon's evolving poetry, at once concise and generous.

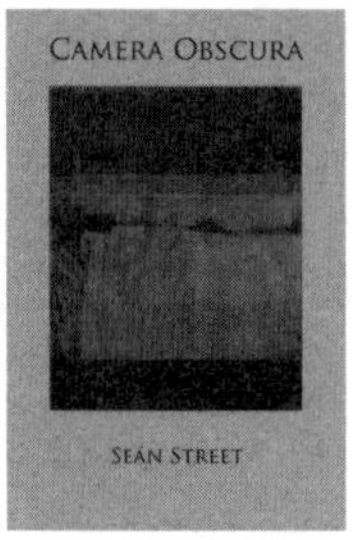

A Message Here

Seán Street, *Camera Obscura*
Rockingham Press, 2016
£9.99

Reviewed by KEVIN J. GARDNER

Recently retired as emeritus professor of radio at Bournemouth University, Seán Street has deftly woven the antithetical arts of poetry and radio broadcasting into a cohesive career. His publications include the original poetry collection *Radio and Other Poems*, the edited collection *Radio Waves: Celebrating the Wireless*, and some six prose works on the history and aesthetics of radio, including *The Poetry of Radio* and *The Memory of Sound*. His longstanding interest in how sound triggers memory is evident in *Camera Obscura*, his ninth poetry collection. An emerging pattern is the capacity for communication across time, witnessed most remarkably in his long central poem, 'The Calderstones', in which the speaker, for whom the titular stones are an enigma of prehistory, dialogues with a Neolithic figure who finds profound spiritual meaning in them.

Our buried dead
tease bewilderment with these shapes,
etch each of us a message here.

Consistent with his interest in radio documentary, dramatic monologue proves a fertile form: Street's subjects include a medieval cathedral mason who witnessed the signing of the Magna Carta, Robert Schumann in the throes of compositional inspiration, the last surviving Beothuk native of Newfoundland, Coleridge's physician interrupting the composition of 'Kubla Khan', the 'bird-man' Léo Valentin plummeting to his death, and even the last wild Tarpan mare of Ukraine, in similar plummet.

Camera Obscura rings with music and sound. Unsurprisingly, Street often thinks in metaphors of recording and broadcasting technologies: short wave, radar, shellac, reel-to-reel, and live wireless broadcast find the language of poetry. Proleptically witty, Street places a sound engineer at the bloody battlefield of

Towton in 1461 ('The Catastrophe Tapes'). Again, Street emphasises the unknowable past, with an accompanying perception that human failings are ever the same:

High pitched screams sounding like feedback,
panic compounded by decay,
distortion, meaningless chaos,
we returned to the same problems
[...]
        incompatibility
of formats, tantalising, strange.

No less tantalising is a musical motif, encompassing not only the aforementioned Schumann but also Elgar, a group of American blues legends, the ninth-symphony phenomenon, and a Schubert mass transformed into poetry.

Street's forms tend to be loose, but noteworthy exceptions can be found in the remarkable Schumann sestina, 'Ghost Variations', and his accentual tetrameter quatrains in 'The Calderstones'. He has a playful taste for anachronism, on display in 'Richard Jefferies on the Diving Board', and an intense eye for natural description, as evident in 'Toad's Mouth'. His title may seem surprising, given his predilection for aural media and metaphor. However, he may be sharing John Locke's notion of the 'dark chamber' whose tiny aperture admitting light and image reflects the nature of human understanding. As Street writes in 'The Art of Falling Slowly',

No such thing as a fixed horizon,
but the grace of light
held for a moment, the art of it.

These lines embody my own impression of this highly accomplished collection.

Quality of Attention

Peter Makin, *Neck of the Woods*
Isobar Press, 2015
£10

Reviewed by TIMOTHY HARRIS

Peter Makin is the author of excellent critical books on Ezra Pound and Basil Bunting, as well as editor of *Basil Bunting on Poetry*, which collects two series of lectures delivered by Bunting (containing some of the best observations on rhythm in English poetry that I know). In his introduction to the latter, Makin quotes Pound's definition of prosody as 'the total articulation of the sound of a poem', expresses his dislike of what he calls 'the bastard form called the "iambic pentameter"', and asserts, with Bunting, that it is rhythm that first of all gives coherence and 'shape' to a poem, anything that goes beyond this, such as the ostentatious patterning of sounds (alliteration, assonance, 'the jingling sound of like endings'), being unnecessary decoration.

Striking metaphors and an excess of adjectives are also unnecessary decoration, and in that same introduction Makin draws attention to two remarks of Bunting: 'Ford (Madox Ford) at his best names *things* and lets them evoke the emotion without mentioning it'; and 'Adjectives mostly weaken the noun they stand with and poetry with too many of them loses its energy and its touch with the world we feel and see.' Decoration of whatever kind blurs the focus, one might say, drawing attention from the object to virtuosity of execution or to feelings entertained, or advertised as being entertained, by the observer, and making the latter more important. Language should be thought of as, ideally, transparent, letting the world in its quiddity shine through. And verse that is written in this way, to quote from Makin's *Pound's Cantos*, 'seems to demonstrate that emotion works by a negative law: mere absence of aggression, distortion, haste allows us to read into things (qualified only as to texture, shade and other exact physicality) powers that favour human well-being'.

Writing verse is seen, therefore, as a discipline which is as much ethical as it is artistic – or rather, the artistic and the ethical become one. I am not convinced that language, or any artistic medium, is transparent in the way Ford, Pound, and Bunting seem to have hoped it was, but what surely can be transmitted by the kind of verse they advocate is, as Makin suggests, not so much the world itself as an attentiveness to it, an attentiveness that because it is reticent and resolutely unsentimental can, like Rubens's portraits of his children, be profoundly moving. It is the quality of the attention in Makin's poems that make them so good.

Attentiveness is not something that exists independent of technique, rather it is created through technique, and it is by means of the care with which Makin's poems are articulated that the quality of attention towards the objects named and described is created and emotion evoked. Attention *is* feeling. Makin is justly dissatisfied with the ideas of traditional prosodists and – to my and Donald Davie's mind – less justly dissatisfied with the pentameter line (rather than with some of its users), but he has a profound, and properly physical, understanding of English prosody, traditional and modern, in Pound's and Bunting's sense of the term. It is an understanding that informs his admirable free verse, which has nothing of what one too often comes across: the slack progression, phrase by banal phrase, haltingly down the page, with occasional words set off in portentous isolation. Instead, there is lively movement shaped by syntax, line-length, spacing, variety of focus and register, and telling enjambment.

The twig knuckle being caught
lifts up a curl of clear water;
ancient of days.

A small pulse, irregular,

down this groove

arising from the play of water-flow
round the leaves and the brown cedar-spray
as they sway
caught under water...

That is the opening of the title-poem, 'Neck of the Woods', which makes up the third of six sections in this collection. The other five sections are the autobiographical *Life-Sketch*; *Hagoromo* ('feather mantle', after the folk-tale and Noh play); *Percepticules* (a collection of haiku-like perceptions); the miscellany *Shore-wrack*; and finally *Ato* ('trace' or 'track', whose Japanese character is homophonous with another character meaning 'afterwards'), dedicated to Makin's wife, Stella Irene Correa, who died in 1997. The collection gathers, we are informed, all the poems from the period 2000–2015 that the poet wishes to preserve.

The neck of the woods in which Makin has lived for many years is a mountain valley north of Kyoto. It is a place of many waters, visited by storms and typhoons; and water and its various movements fascinate the poet, and have always fascinated him, judging from the childhood memory of Lincolnshire that opens the collection:

Clean clearwater sand
out beyond the rubble and the shore-wrack

a thin stream
cutting its own bed as you diverted it
tiny sharp grains
on inside bends,
forking across plains

half a centimetre
in unmarked sand...

But in *Hagoromo*, the water is menacing and destructive, even as the poet seeks to create a Horatian monument to his wife *quod non imber edax* [...] *possit diruere*:

Under the thick sheet of water
ribbed, rushing
an eye of air

A scattering of thin silver cigarette foils
on the black ash, like paper to the touch now they've been burned.
On the heap of rice-straw mats; then the flood from the typhoon took them [...]

Tears, too, are water. The attentiveness is underlain by loss, the particulars by the void, which is all in the end there is and 'which is filled / with these things temporarily'. The sense of desolation in these poems is at times overpowering, and the more so because of the fineness, concentration, and liveliness of the perceptions:

The ink puckers the paper
at the knots where the brush turned,
pulling the strength in.

There is a splendid muscularity there, the lines seeming to reproduce in yet another medium the movement of the now-vanished hand and arm that is recorded on the paper – calligraphy, perhaps, or an ink-painting? (I have seen Japanese people standing before a landscape painting by Hasegawa Tohaku, rehearsing the movements the painter must have made.) For beyond, or under, the fascination with water, there is a fascination with movement of every kind, and with creating the physical feeling of these movements in the forms of verse. There is also a fascination with qualities of light, with colours, with smells, and with sounds: the cawing of crows, the 'clear plop' of the nightingale, the soughing 'of a thousand trees, range to range, as the darkness closes', 'the little low beat' that turns out to be the train to Kinosaki, 'tiny waterpattering', bamboos grinding against each other in the wind, the thwock of a mallet, the 'deer-shriek'... And the water everywhere, the humidity, the oppressive closeness of the trees, the wild boars, the *tanuki* – one ends this collection feeling a profound intimacy with this densely wooded valley where the poet notices, in his Japanese Hippocrene,

Strange regularities
in the burrowing of the creatures
in the soft mud under the water
where I drink my drink for my
dead wife and wash my face.

Being and Neverness

Sean Ashton, *Living in a Land*
Eros Press, 2016
£6

Reviewed by NICOLAS TREDELL

An epigraph from Sartre's *Being and Nothingness* precedes the 148-page monologue that constitutes Sean Ashton's novel *Living in a Land*: 'It would be in vain to deny that negation appears on the original basis of a relation of man to the world. The world does not disclose its non-beings to one who has not first posited them as possibilities.' Sartre's existentialism stressed self-creation by action, by what one does, but acknowledged that one also defines oneself by inaction, by what one does not do. Ashton's novel offers a speaker who constructs himself primarily by negation, by telling us what he never has and never will do.

'Never', in literature and life, is often the adverb of loss, finality, or regret. We have, for example, Lear's fivefold recognition that Cordelia will not come again ('Never, never, never, never, never'); the remorseless reiterations of Poe's eponymous raven quothing 'Nevermore'; the lost possibility of fulfilment in Eliot's 'Burnt Norton' ('the door we never opened / Into the rose-garden'); the failure to conform to the pattern of a Lawrencian *Bildungsroman* in Larkin's 'I Remember, I Remember' ('that splendid family / I never ran to when I got depressed' and 'the bracken where I never trembling sat'). But *Living in a Land* is no elegy; it does not suggest the speaker regrets those things he has left undone or will not do.

Ashton's monologue relies much on anaphora and grammatical parallelism. His most prominent way of starting a sentence is: 'I've never', as in this passage:

> I've never had to reach for the hammer or the cordless, or do the best I can with the heaviest object to hand and the nearest thing to a nail. I've never gone outward bound. I've never given anyone sage advice. I've never given anyone a piece of my mind. I've never given anyone a blow job.

Ashton also employs 'never' in the present tense, as in 'I never watch TV during the daytime' and the future tense, 'I shall never', as in 'I shall never try to impress waiters or curry favour with plumbers'. Other negative sentence-starts include 'I no longer', as in 'I no longer pay attention to the changing of the seasons'; 'It is surely inconceivable', as in 'It is surely inconceivable that people will soon demand a vegetarian option at my barbecue when no such precedent has ever been set'; 'I am not persuaded', as in 'I am not persuaded that our friendship in its current format is worth preserving'; 'I am not convinced', as in 'I am not convinced that the scansion of Anglican hymns is all it could be'; 'I forgo', as in 'I forgo surveys, customer feedback forms, questionnaires, multiple-choice tests'; 'I have little confidence', as in 'I have little confidence we shall locate the transponder'; and 'it seems [or 'is'] unlikely', as in 'It is unlikely, now, that I shall ever follow in the footsteps of Hercules'.

Like Christine Brooke-Rose or Georges Perec, Ashton works within his self-imposed constraints with energy, wit and inventiveness; *Living in a Land* offers a refreshing alternative to the burnished banalities of a Barnes or McEwan. But it also provides an implicit diagnosis of both the proliferation and constriction of possibilities in the way we live now, facing a profusion of 'lifestyle choices' which are in fact closely circumscribed and which never touch the real. While Sartre supplies its epigraph, Ashton's novel maps a land – or is it a hedonistic hell? – in which one will never find a key Sartrean component: authenticity.

Hate / Love

Ben Lerner, *The Hatred of Poetry*
Farrar, Straus and Giroux, 2016
$12

Reviewed by DAVID C. WARD

That Ben Lerner's little book has excited attention even outside Poetry World is down to the shock of its title: *The Hatred of Poetry*. Who hates poetry, you ask? And 'Hate' is so categorical and extreme that it brings you up short. Which, of course, it is designed to do. *The Hatred of Poetry* is a polemical essay in the tradition of the great pamphlet literature of the eighteenth or nineteenth century. If not *J'accuse*, it is certainly a *What is to be done?* about poetry, both for poets and their audience. Although his diagnosis is stringent, Lerner is not quite a revolutionary, both because he is too tentative temperamentally but also because he has no prescription or programme for poetry to follow. He wants us to examine our assumptions about poetry, both the writing and the reading of it.

Hatred is a hard emotion to sustain and Lerner's commitment to its adamancy begins to waver from the outset; again, he's no revolutionary. Lerner begins with an anecdote about how as a school child he was forced to memorise a chunk of poetry and mischievously chose Marianne Moore's 'Poetry' with its line about poetry, 'I, too, dislike it.' Well, dislike is a distance away from hate. Those people who pay attention to poetry (a lot of people don't, of course) don't hate poetry, rather the obverse: they love it, perhaps too much, because they expect too much of it. No one indicts the novel as a form because every year huge numbers of potboilers across all genres, from romances to spy stories or mysteries, are published for the entertainment of the public; indeed, the argument can and has been made that popular or genre fiction has invigorated the novel both idiomatically and by expanding its cultural range. But trashy poetry is simply not allowed! We hold poetry to the highest standard – and are constantly disappointed, as Lerner is, when it fails – inevitably – to meet our aesthetic, emotional, and intellectual needs. If you hate something, you leave it behind. But we can't quit poetry. And if we don't hate 'it', we also don't dislike 'it' *a la* Moore or the young Lerner. We love Poetry, we dislike poems because they disappoint us.

The distinction between Poetry, as an idealistic concept, and the actual poem is at the centre of the most interesting part of Lerner's essay. He is frustrated by the apparent irreconcilability of what the poet wants to achieve in her mind and what she is then able to produce on the page. Enacting the idea and embodying it in words on the page seems to Lerner to be an epistemologically impossible task. Lerner, glossing an argument by Allen Grossman, writes that 'the poem is always a record of failure' going on to say that the 'abstract potential of the medium as felt by the poet' is then betrayed by the actual poem when it 'joins the world of representation'. Lerner realises the presence of this dichotomy in his own work as a poet: 'like so many poets, I live in the space between what I am moved to do and what I can do, and confront in that disconnect not only my individual limitation [...] but also the structure of the art as I conceive it'. The limit case of Lerner's use of the word hate is Plato, who actually did hate poetry because he thought it was a threat to the Republic 'because poets are rhetoricians who pass off imaginative projections as truth and risk corrupting the citizens of the just city'. What Lerner would actually like is not to share Plato's hatred but to achieve what the philosopher feared: the absolute and frightening colonisation of the real world by the poet's imagination.

The problem for Lerner's polemic is that having introduced Plato and a very interesting philosophical (or even neurological) dilemma, he then goes off on a pretty formulaic discussion of how and why poetry has been criticised over the years for the ways that it disappoints us. This just re-states Lerner's premise: Poetry, not poems. What one senses as one reads Lerner is that he actually would prefer writing a cultural or critical history of poetry's reception. As he says at one point, people prefer to quote or cite lines of poems rather than poems in their entirety. Poetry, in other words, is used – used to make a point about something else. A poetry quote is a trump card to buttress or win an argument. A poetry quote heightens the tone and adds dignity or gravitas to otherwise mundane human activities like funerals or presidential inaugurations. Poetry has a privileged, almost untouchable status in public culture to the point that it has become ossified: people don't actually listen to it anymore. It's Poetry, so the words don't matter.

Lerner wants us passionately to re-engage with poetry to the point where we will actually hate its failures, instead of simply – blah blah blah Poetry – hear the words go in one ear and out the other. Lerner's 'Hate' is forlorn: he wants poetry in and of itself to become so important that like Plato it can be hated. Given contemporary culture, particularly in America, where authority has become more decentralised and our attention spans seem to have shrunk, it's hard to see this happening. But Lerner is entitled to his ambitions for poetry, and his polemic, despite its wavering attention span, might cause at least some of us invested in poetry to think a little more carefully about what we want for poetry and how we find it.

Pebbles

David Morley, *The Death of Wisdom Smith, Prince of Gypsies*, Melos, £5; Alison Winch, *Trouble*, Emma Press, £6; Rosemary Norman, *For Example*, Shoestring, £9; Todd Swift, *Madness & Love in Maida Vale*, Eyewear, £5; Mary King, *Homing*, smith/doorstop, £5; Paul Deaton, *Black Knight*, Eyewear, £5; Stephanie Conn, *Copeland's Daughter*, smith/doorstop, £5; Judith Wilkinson & Ditty Doornbos *Canyon Journey*, Shoestring, £9; Suzanna Fitzpatrick, *Fledglings*, Red Squirrel, £6; Elizabeth Parker, *Antinopolis*, Eyewear, £5; Geoff Gilbert & Alex Houen, *Hold! West*, Eyewear, £5; Cal Freeman, *Heard Among the Windbreak*, Eyewear, £5

Reviewed by ALISON BRACKENBURY

The steady trickle of pamphlets into the *PN Review* office has swelled to a flood! Let me aim a few quick pebbles over the stream.

The Death of Wisdom Smith, Prince of Gypsies, opens with a cascade of caravans: 'Laverock All Alone of all the Crafters / Northward and Sherebiah of the Nails'... Ecstatic and elegiac, Romani names return at intervals, like waves: 'of the Englands   no word'. 'Not one baker sleeps' while supplying Wisdom's funeral, its 'vardos [caravans] with wheel-rims lulled in sackcloth'. Do not be lulled; there are twists in this stream. Many poems flow. David Morley's catch the shock and spray of fresh water. I will toss in one tiny pebble of fact. This story continues. I once met a Romani Princess – on a work experience scheme. Since she had to attend funerals (and weddings) all over Europe, she had trouble keeping jobs...

But *Trouble* may be delicious: 'golden light, muddy crystals, kissing cherries'. If you think, as I do, that there are not enough good poems about sex, read Alison Winch's 'O Kingsland Road. O Bus.' 'Everything's alive: whelks, do-nuts'. Even her syntax seethes. A joyful plunge into Middle English brings 'poppys and primeroles' and the 'newte [...] not myne but its own self's the leaves' the sky's'. The best writing about the body is generous. Like Winch's work, it flows out into the world – which, in *Trouble*, also includes 'cabbage-green' pregnancy sickness, and the 'milk pudding feet' of age.

Rosemary Norman confronts age in the spare, tough poems of *For Example*: 'Let me take / your stick / & hearing aid & / glasses   so the young man / here can cut / your hair   then we'll go / for cakes and coffee'. Her unsentimental flow of speech seems straightforward as swift swimming. Both are extremely skilled. So is Norman's apparent simplicity at her poems' end: 'and the old, sweet chill / at the sea's edge / still has him by the ankles.'

In Todd Swift's opening poem, 'Christ, Swimming' is a man of 'blood and oxygen', a carpenter 'drowned on the cross'. It is a sustained, passionate and practical hymn, warmly linked to the flow of daily life, where Christ becomes 'our captain of the swimming team'. The best poems in *Madness & Love in Maida Vale* are the most controlled, like 'Ash, Wednesday': 'My father, in his coffin [...] His stillness in the midst of things.'

In the midst of human life, Mary King's *Homing* shows intense sympathy with birds. She describes a French bluetit battering a window: '*Pauvre petit oiseau, tout le jour*, the concierge says.' King concludes: 'We too lose heart, too late, too late.' Her patient account of a godwit's migration flares to life at the moments when her description of the bird could, touchingly, be that of a person: 'At the edge of the tide, / under a scrubby bush, / she is asleep.'

Paul Deaton's *Black Knight* displays an appealing talent for isolating scenes and objects from life's onward rush. In the title poem, a Monopoly set is memorably 'yanked by a seaman uncle from his sinking merchant ship / U-boat torpedoed.' Deaton's verbs – and colours – are arresting: 'Some burly blacksmith / has quenched the sun / in the cold sea of the sky, / the cherry flames, distant, intensify.'

Copeland's Daughter is Stephanie Conn's careful account of the lives of ancestors on islands in the north Irish Sea. Conn notes that there can be 'nothing ornamental' in a garden perilously close to waves. Her own poems remain fittingly plain. They are most lyrical about food: 'the creamy sunshine' of newly-made butter. They are most fluent when describing sea, as in the action of a coracle: 'heave, sway, bob'. Conn's austere use of fact is bitterly effective when her family's island life ends: 'Out in the yard / they are selling our lives.'

Canyon Journey is based on living experience of ME (Chronic Fatigue Symptom), reflected in Ditty Doornbos's art and Judith Wilkinson's poems. Illness is translated memorably into desert landscapes: 'It was the oldest night [...] I started walking towards the unreachable distance.' The reader is rewarded by rain, although, finally, 'the canyon stays'.

In contrast, Suzanna Fitzpatrick's *Fledglings* offers one of the strongest re-creations of pregnancy I have read, 'telling an old, old story / like the freshest news', including morning sickness, 'as we tumble to our knees, snatch back our hair'.

Elizabeth Parker's *Antinopolis* takes its title from an Egyptian city named after an Emperor's drowned favourite. The poems mix a heady cocktail of beauty and violence. The speaker in 'Wife' picks up a dress: 'her silk waist clenched / in the tube of my fist'. Parker's best lines bristle with energy: 'Let the breeze in, sister.'

I tried to breeze through *Hold! West* three times. I skimmed. Then I sank. Finally, I floated. Geoff Gilbert and Alex Houen's list of 'careful and intensive shared reading' embraces novels and philosophy. Take a dip, reader. First, 'the construction of the child's social world'. Collaged quotation? Then an arabesque of wild humour: 'there is not a child / anywhere in Europe who doesn't have lovers, horses, cars'. The poems' tides carry vivid literal vignettes. The Iron Curtain is 'a tall metallic wall'. Soldiers (or death) descend from a line's end: 'the guest-worker falls / from the ladder'. We finally land on an 'elevation' [...] so I could touch once more a world / of solid people making up their minds'. Do these poems, with their 'immaculate Europa', their often baffling mental excess, seem too elevated after so many British voters made up their minds to leave the EU? But Europe's history sweeps through *Hold! West* in complex tides of ideas. 'Will there also be singing?' Brecht asked, in the *Svendborg Poems*; 'Yes, there will also be singing / About the dark times.' And, as Gilbert and Houen suggest, there will also be thinking – and the memory of yoghurt: 'thick bright milk in a glass pot'.

Cal Freeman draws on different memories in 'the post-industrial watersheds of Southeast Michigan'. Like Winch and Fitzpatrick, he considers the 'preposterous' body, and 'the same retching our mothers / once mistook for love'. Freeman's Michigan can be both elemental and engagingly contemporary: 'She wears a Gore-Tex anorak to bear / the heavy rain that's falling from the north'. He is a keen explorer of regions of the mind 'as if this town were the geometry of grief / and we were blameless'. But the urgent title poem of *Heard Among the Windbreak* is set in an all too real place, where 'the bedrock fractures'. Here are fracking and its impure streams. 'In the shadow of a derrick / this is bitterness and home.' Freeman's tiny savage half-rhymes take the pulse of a landscape with 'backflow ditches / where the heron drink and sicken'. It is a superb poem, which hovers above the polluted waters like Freeman's own 'mourning doves'. The collection ends with an extraordinary vision of an aftermath 'as the eohippus starts to gallop / over this fallow ground again'. There is more anger, compassion and technical authority in this pamphlet than in many full collections. Snatch it from the stream.

From the Archive

Issue 132, March - April 2000

RAFAEL ALBERTI
translated by Anthony Edkins

Fellow contributors to this issue include Anne Stevenson, Alison Brackenbury, Jeremy Over, Robert Bly, Jeremy Hooker, Ruth Padel, and Christopher Middleton.

YOU ARE A DISASTER

You are a disaster
or an open sky where a rainbow is installed.
Of you, everything is expected.
Facing the sea, naked
someone recently risen from shipwreck,
you are covered with winds and bad weather
and the stone you project
can as likely break flower's eye
as baby start
or bird or star.

Become a subscriber and gain unlimited online access to the entire *PN Review* archive spanning over forty years.

SOME CONTRIBUTORS

Linda Anderson is Professor of English and Director of the Newcastle Centre for the Literary Arts at Newcastle University. She is the author of numerous critical books including *Elizabeth Bishop: Lines of Connection* (EUP) and a poetry pamphlet with Mariscat, *Greenhouse* (2013). Gabriella Attems studied Comparative Literature in Vienna and Organic Horticulture in Ireland. Her translations of Charles Bernstein were among the recipients of the City of Münster Poetry Prize 2015. **Tara Bergin** is from Dublin. Her first collection of poems, *This is Yarrow*, was published by Carcanet in 2013. **Caroline Bird** has four collections published with Carcanet, most recently 'The Hat-Stand Union.' She won a major Eric Gregory award in 2002 and has been shortlisted twice for The Dylan Thomas Prize. She is currently writing the book and lyrics for 'Dennis the Menace the Musical' for The Old Vic Theatre, and working on her fifth poetry collection. **Ross Cogan** has a PhD in logic. He has won a Gregory Award and published two collections with Oversteps. A freelance writer, he is Creative Director of the Cheltenham Poetry Festival. **Ned Denny**'s poems have appeared in magazines including Poetry Review, the *TLS*, *Oxford Poetry* and *PN Review*. He is currently working on a 900-stanza poem titled *B*, a recreation of the Divine Comedy. **P.C. Evans** has published poetry and translations of Dutch drama, poetry and fiction. His latest publication is the forthcoming pamphlet *Cadaver Dog Cantos* (KFS Press), for which he received a Literature Wales Bursary. **Adam Feinstein** is a poet, translator and author of the acclaimed biography *Pablo Neruda: A Passion for Life*, re-issued in an updated edition by Bloomsbury in 2013. It has been translated into a number of languages, including Chinese. **Isabel Galleymore**'s debut pamphlet is *Dazzle Ship* (Worple Press, 2014). Her work has featured in Poetry Review, Poetry London, and in 2016 she won the Jane Martin Poetry Prize and the Basil Bunting Award. She is currently preparing for a writing residency in the Peruvian Amazon. **Jodie Hollander**'s full length collection, *My Dark Horses*, is due out with Liverpool University Press (Pavilion Poetry) in April 2017. **Mary Noonan**'s first collection – *The Fado House* (Dedalus, 2012) – was shortlisted for the Seamus Heaney Centre Prize and the Strong/Shine Award. A pamphlet, *Father* (Bonnefant Press) was published in 2015. **Gregory O'Brien**, a poet, painter and curator, was Stout Memorial Fellow at Victoria University of Wellington, 2015-16, during which time he completed a book exploring the relationship between the imagination and the environment. **Vidyan Ravinthiran** teaches at Durham University. His debut, *Grun-tu-molani* (Bloodaxe, 2014), was shortlisted for multiple first collection awards, including the Forward. He is also co-editor of *Prac Crit*, the online magazine of poetry and poetics, and *Elizabeth Bishop's Prosaic*, his study of that poet, appeared in 2015. **Grant Shipcott** has run XL Publishing Services for some thirty years, setting 120 issues of *PN Review*, as well as hundreds of poetry collections and academic books and journals. www.xlpublishingservices.co.uk. **Mark Thompson** first wrote for *PNR* about William Empson in 1984. *Birth Certificate: The Story of Danilo Kiš* won the Jan Michalski Prize (2015) and the Laura Shannon Prize (2016). **Jeffrey Wainwright**'s seventh Carcanet collection, *What Must Happen*, was published in July 2016. He is also the author of *Poetry: The Basics* and *Acceptable Words: Essays on the Poetry of Geoffrey Hill*. **Gina Wilson**'s pamphlet collection *Scissors, Paper, Stone* was published by Happenstance in 2010. She has also authored *Jim-Jam Pyjamas* (Cape), a poetry collection for children, as well as novels for young adults. Her novel *Cora Ravenwing* was reissued by Faber Finds in 2013.

COLOPHON

Editors
Michael Schmidt (General)
Luke Allan (Deputy)

Design
Luke Allan
2016

Type
PN Review is set in Arnhem, a typeface designed by Fred Smeijers in 1999.

Editorial address
The Editors at the address on the right. Manuscripts cannot be returned unless accompanied by a stamped addressed envelope or international reply coupon.

Subscriptions (6 issues)
individuals: £39/$86
institutions: £49/$105
to: PN Review, Alliance House
30 Cross Street, Manchester
M2 7AQ, UK

Represented by
Compass Independent Publishing Services Ltd
Great West House, Great West Road
Brentford TW8 9DF, UK
sales@compass-ips.london

Trade distributors
NBN International
10 Thornbury Road
Plymouth PL6 7PP, UK
orders@nbninternational.com

Copyright
© 2016 Poetry Nation Review
All rights reserved
ISBN 978-1-78410-143-5
ISSN 0144-7076

Supported by
Supported using public funding by
ARTS COUNCIL ENGLAND